HOW TO MANAGE BEHAVIOUR IN FURTHER EDUCATION

DAVE VIZARD

HOW TO MANAGE BEHAVIOUR
IN FURTHER EDUCATION

AGE RANGE 16+

PHOTOCOPIABLE RESOURCES

Los Angeles | London | New Delhi
Singapore | Washington DC

2ND EDITION

First edition published 2007

This edition first published 2012

SAGE Publications Ltd
1 Oliver's Yard
55 City Road
London EC1Y 1SP

SAGE Publications Inc.
2455 Teller Road
Thousand Oaks, California 91320

SAGE Publications India Pvt Ltd
B 1/I 1 Mohan Cooperative Industrial Area
Mathura Road
New Delhi 110 044

SAGE Publications Asia-Pacific Pte Ltd
3 Church Street
#10-04 Samsung Hub
Singapore 049483

Library of Congress Control Number: 2011938956

British Library Cataloguing in Publication data

A catalogue record for this book is available from the British Library

ISBN 978-1-4462-0282-1
ISBN 978-1-4462-0283-8 (pbk)

Typeset by C&M Digitals (P) Ltd, Chennai, India
Printed in India at Replika Press Pvt Ltd
Printed on paper from sustainable resources

CONTENTS

Dave Vizard is an independent consultant who regularly trains lecturers, teachers and support workers around the country on behaviour management. His years of experience in the field translate into realistic, and frequently entertaining, advice.

Dave has worked at Plymouth University on the foundation degree and trains extensively throughout the UK in FE colleges. He has had 39 years of experience in education in a variety of settings. He has also trained trainers for the Learning and Skills Network (formerly the Learning and Skills Development Agency) in Behaviour Management. Dave has set up his own consultancy company, Behaviour Solutions, to provide staff training and development for schools and FE colleges.

For more information about other publications by the author, a free newsletter, and information about quality staff development provided by Behaviour Solutions, visit Dave's website at **www. behavioursolutions.com**

ACKNOWLEDGEMENTS

Thanks to my family, Annwyn, Emma and Tim, for all their support, and in particular to my wife Annwyn who gave me so much encouragement and help in producing this book and without whose support none of this would have been possible. Special thanks should also be extended to all the staff in the Further Education Colleges with whom I have worked over many years and in particular to:

Lee Hughes

Pamela Willerton (Community Based First Aid and Resilience, Devon)

Adrian Turnpenny (Doncaster College)

Helen Colledge (Petroc, Barnstaple)

Sam Booth (Petroc, Barnstaple)

Gordon Finlay (Bicton College)

Perwez Iqbal (City College, Birmingham)

CHAPTER 1

Getting started

Context – understanding the diverse range of learners' backgrounds and experiences

Students today are coming from more diverse backgrounds and with a variety of different experiences and this makes managing their behaviour in FE establishments more challenging. Teaching in what was a post-compulsory sector now involves working with compulsory school-aged students either in a college setting or in a school setting (Wolf Report, 2011). Students arriving direct from school at the age of 16 bring with them a range of challenges. Many learners find it difficult to handle the expectations of FE and have difficulty in studying independently having been spoon-fed in schools. The proportion of learners arriving with Special or Additional Needs is also increasing. Recent government findings (DfE, 2010a) stated that 21 per cent of pupils in schools had Special Needs which was nearly double the figure given in 1990. Behaviour and speech problems represent the fastest growing categories. Ten per cent of pupils with Special Needs have statements.

Many older learners will be returning to learning for a variety of reasons. Some will have been encouraged by employers to take a range of courses to improve their qualifications and in a number of cases these learners can be somewhat reluctant. High levels of unemployment have led to adults attending courses to improve their qualifications, skill levels and employability. Some of these older learners will have a range of learning and behavioural difficulties. Many lecturers are teaching on courses with mixed age and experience groups – very young students together with older learners – which can pose a significant challenge as well. In addition, working with young offenders and in prison education can present various problems where there are clearly different expectations. Land-based study and work in practical areas will also often create challenges.

Causes of challenging behaviour

- *Poor previous learning experiences*

    ○ Many learners have incredibly low self-esteem because of the many negative experiences they have had.

- ○ 'Factory farming' – testing from the age of 5 has led to some learners dis-engaging from the learning process and displaying challenging behaviour as a way of gaining recognition.

- ○ Lack of differentiation with tasks that lack challenge.

- ○ Poor relationships with staff.

- *Adapting to college life*

  - ○ Unable to cope with size of college and large number of students.

  - ○ Inability to manage unsupervised time.

  - ○ Frightened of being challenged and being taken out of comfort zone and away from former peer group.

- *Home background*

  - ○ Many parents do not have the necessary parenting skills and so will not have provided appropriate levels of nurturing in the early years or effective support mechanisms.

  - ○ The breakdown of the family unit has meant that many students do not have appropriate role models and sometimes have aggressive role models.

  - ○ Some students turn to gangs for support as they offer safety and a sense of identity. Many are also under immense pressure from their peer group. Anti-social behaviour for some groups is seen as 'a badge of honour': for example, drinking, using abusive and threatening behaviour, or damaging/graffitying property. This can be further extended to drug taking and promiscuous/sexual activity. Many students feel pressurised – they must join in or become a victim.

- *Mental health issues*

  - ○ Mental health issues are a real concern. The *Good Childhood Inquiry* (The Children's Society, 2008) stated that mental health problems were on the increase and described the situation as a mental health epidemic, with severe emotional and psychological distress common.

- *Crime*

  - ○ Vizard (2009: 4) stated that those in gangs 'are enmeshed in crime and that over 70% of offenders in London are under the age of 18 … crime means little – it is an unexceptional event'.

- *Substance abuse*

  - ○ One piece of research by Greenfield (2007) illustrated the extent of drug use where 12 per cent of 11- to 15-year-olds had used cannabis and 4 per cent had used Class A drugs such as heroin.

- *Television/media/internet*

    ○ Students come to college disrupted because of the images they see on television in news bulletins and the violent themes in some 'soaps'. Some of the topics on radio can also be quite disturbing, as can the lyrics to certain songs.

    ○ Easy access to films on DVD can lead to students seeing disturbing and aggressive content.

    ○ Some video games are quite violent and can have a desensitising effect on people which will limit their capacity for empathy – thereby causing people to become unnaturally violent when faced with challenges.

    ○ Easy access to very disturbing images on the internet can be distressing.

- *Food for thought*

    ○ Some students do not re-hydrate sufficiently: each of us should drink approximately 1.2 litres of water per day (Food Standards Agency, 2006). In addition students who consume coffee and other drinks with a high caffeine content can experience a diuretic effect. As the brain is made up of more than 80 per cent water (Blakemore and Frith, 2005: 18), and uses 30 per cent of all the water a person consumes (Vizard, 2004a: 6), dehydration can have a severe impact on behaviour and the ability to learn.

    ○ Many of the fast foods and ready prepared food items that some students consume are full of additives which can severely affect their behaviour. With the recession, more processed foods which can contain high levels of additives are now being consumed.

    ○ Increasing students' intake of fish oil supplements can improve their behaviour and learning (see further Blakemore and Frith, 2005: 186).

    ○ Increasing students' zinc and iron intake has also been shown to improve their behaviour (see further Northern, 2004).

Reflection on practice

A number of causes for challenging behaviour have been given above. For any two of these look at a couple of interventions you could provide to overcome the negative impact of these areas. Then discuss these with a partner.

Cause 1

1 _____

_____

2 _____

_____

(Continued)

(Continued)

Cause 2

1 _____
_____

2 _____
_____

Research on brain reconfiguration in adolescence and its effect on learning and behaviour

Prior to birth and throughout our lives our brain cells will undergo pruning. Giedd (2004, cited in Wallis, 2004) suggested that at the age of 11 in girls and 12 ½ years in boys a key period of massive pruning takes place which will then continue until around the age of 25. During this time the adolescent pre-frontal cortex will be smaller than that found in younger children. Some brain areas will shrink back to allow others maximum resources whilst they develop. During this phase adolescents will be unable to show empathy and will often give inappropriate responses. Because of this pruning and change in configuration, adolescents:

- are very impulsive

- love risk taking because this generates rushes of the hormone dopamine

- cannot easily assess the causes and effects of their actions

- are less able to assess threats

- are ruled by their emotions more than logic

- are unable to recover from trauma easily.

The area of the brain that reconfigures first is the part that controls sensory preference – the visual, auditory, kinaesthetic, olfactory and gustatory. As the brain reconfigures the more rational regions of the upper cortex we see the following:

- The development of attributes associated with maturity.

- A calmer outlook.

- Stable moods.

- A decrease in risk taking.

- The ability to reason and think things through.

When the pre-frontal cortex is reconfigured students will be more able to do the following:

- Plan.

- Set priorities.

- Organise their thoughts.

- Suppress their impulses.

- Weigh up the consequences of their actions.

There is a later maturation of the frontal lobes in Western society because of a longer period of dependency upon parents and the associated abdication of adult responsibilities. Many students will have 'helicopter parents', those who will hover over their children doing everything for them. Young people are now staying at home longer because of higher living costs and the scarcity of jobs, and due to the increases in tuition fees, many will attend local Higher Education Institutions to save on accommodation costs. However, we can see an early maturation of the frontal lobes in young adults in other societies due to their having to assume adult responsibilities at a much earlier age.

Reflection on practice

With a partner discuss the following:

1   How could you adapt your teaching strategies to take account of the information on brain reconfiguration in adolescence?

   _____
   _____
   _____
   _____

2   How would you manage the behaviour of learners given the information above relating to their impulsivity and lack of empathy?

   _____
   _____
   _____
   _____

Academic versus vocational groups and issues of teaching combined groups

The range of abilities across and within groups can cause a real challenge to most lecturers. Often you have to meet combined groups made up of students on vocational and academic courses. Making an appropriate differentiation can be a problem and also the types of behaviour displayed can be different. More able students can often undermine others in the group. In addition, some of the students on vocational courses, who are there because they have been told to enrol on a course, can often behave in an inappropriate manner by using bad language and making extremely negative comments to other learners. Managing these groups effectively is a real challenge. Sessions will often need to be fast-paced and students will have to be re-grouped using a number of co-operative learning techniques. A clear understanding of expectations and boundaries will also need to be established.

With some vocational groups it can be difficult to keep students onside due to boredom on their part. Many will be accustomed to fast-paced environments. Some will be taking courses because it is an employer requirement that they gain certain qualifications. Often there will be a reluctance on their part as they do not want to be in college. If such students are proving to be a challenge then a letter to their employer or using peer pressure can help to halt this.

Students on academic courses can often present challenges of a different kind. Within groups students' understanding of the work can vary dramatically making any differentiation between learners extremely difficult. Some may find the work difficult: for example, on an accountancy course the technical dimension of this subject means that some students will struggle and as a result they may display behaviour which is untypical – their attendance deteriorates, they will use distraction techniques, or they will become quiet and withdrawn. Meanwhile other learners may display arrogance because they have an inflated opinion about their ability. As a result of this, students in these groups will test a lecturer's knowledge of the subject and be very demanding. Being vigilant and checking students' progress are key here. Early intervention is necessary if we notice any change in students: we must be able to offer support or set up a buddying system, for example. With students who frequently challenge our knowledge it is best not to over-react and defer their queries to the end of the session when these can be fully discussed. If we do over-react to frequent queries and challenges this can act as an accelerant to their behaviour. Often when a student frequently interrupts the peer group will often act together to modify their behaviour.

How to understand and engage Additional Needs learners

A number of learners will suffer from several conditions and syndromes and indeed it is not unusual for some students to have three or four conditions. The age of onset and duration will vary from condition to condition. The government's Green Paper on Special Educational Needs and Disabilities in March 2010 re-affirmed the need to support learners in Further Education. Statements of Special Educational Needs are being replaced by Education, Health and Care Plans which aim to help education and health professionals to work together. These plans will be required from birth to the age of 25 for all individuals with Additional Needs.

Characteristics of conditions and strategies to use

Autism

Characteristics

Autistic students spend their time engaged in puzzling and disturbing behaviours. Three areas have been identified:

- Impairment in social interaction.

- Impairment in communication.

- Restricted and repetitive patterns of behaviour.

Diprose and Burge (2003) listed the following characteristics:

- Difficulty in relating to people, events or even objects – isolation is preferred.

- Delays in language and cognitive development – limited intellectual ability.

- Impaired social interaction.

- Unconventional use of toys.

- Avoidance of eye contact.

- Insistence on routine and environment remaining unchanged.

- Repetitive movements – rocking, spinning, head banging.

- Unusual sleep patterns – can stay up all night.

Treatment/strategies

- *Developing communication/language* – this involves helping students to learn various ways to communicate, initially by using sign language and pictures rather than verbal language. Using visual cues/cards is important. Using speech and drama to help with conversation and not keeping thoughts to themselves encourages thinking, teaches students opening comments for conversations, and gets them to ask for help.

- *Social skills* – this involves teaching students to play and share, helping them with their emotional literacy, using co-operative learning, and helping them to understand and express their emotions. Reassurance and praise are also important.

- *Behaviour management* – this involves making the environment structured and predictable. Unstructured time is when problems can arise – so having a structure to the day is needed, time out strategies can also prove useful. When poor behaviour is displayed refer to the rules and insist these are kept. Remain calm and keep the volume down.

- *Motor co-ordination* – this involves exercises and games being developed to help with clumsiness. Writing can also be supported through using keyboards.

Further reading

www.autism.org

www.paains.org.uk

www.wikipedia/org/wiki/Autism

Asperger Syndrome (AS)

Characteristics

Students with AS often have the following characteristics:

- Experience difficulty with social relationships:

  - want to be sociable and enjoy human contact

  - have difficulty in understanding how others feel

  - find it hard to read non-verbal communication including facial expressions

  - find it hard to maintain eye contact

- Find communication difficult:

  - find it difficult to have a two-way conversation, taking all the time to speak without wanting to listen, and they do not check listeners' reactions

  - have difficulty communicating their feelings and reactions to others

  - when faced with a challenge they may run away and hide or vent their frustration through temper or tantrums

  - they can be over-precise and over-literal, with turns of phrase and metaphors causing alarm, and jokes and exaggerated language also creating a problem

- Emotionally fragile:

  - can be self-critical and easily become stressed; some will also have difficulties coping with everyday life; changes in routines and transitions can also be challenging

- Special interests:

  - may develop an almost obsessive interest in a hobby or interest, which involves them arranging or memorising facts about a special subject such as train timetables or football results

- Verbal IQ is lower than performance IQ.

Treatment/strategies

- *There is no specific treatment* – it is however possible for a student with AS to acquire social skills.

- *Teach relaxation techniques using breathing exercises, stress balls* – the demands of adolescence mean a student with AS is likely to be under considerable stress.

- *Establish a clear achievable routine* – use posters to provide visual information.

- *Provide a structured, consistent and predictable environment.*

- *Inform them about changes of teachers and rooms in advance.*

- *Give positive feedback whenever possible.*

- *Use clear language and instructions* – avoid using ambiguity, humour or irony.

- *Build self-esteem* – give positive feedback whenever possible.

- *Encourage use of co-operative learning techniques.*

Attention Deficit Hyperactivity Disorder (ADHD)

Characteristics

Students with ADHD cannot block out the stimuli that constantly surround us (noise, smells and texture). They are continually distracted by them and therefore find it difficult to focus on one task only.

ADHD manifests itself in three main ways:

- Hyperactivity.

- Impulsiveness.

- Inattention.

Treatment/strategies

- *Create a structured, predictable environment* – use consistent seating arrangements, rules, expectations and logical consequences (the consequences of a student's behaviour have to be instant: see Jensen, 2005).

- *Make instructions about behaviour as clear as possible* – give precise instructions starting with the student's name and ensure eye contact. Repeat, using the 'broken record' technique if necessary.

- *Position students in class where they are least likely to be distracted* – sit them away from known distractions.

- *Try to keep the noise level low and prevent distractions.*

- *Break up tasks into attainable steps.*

- *Keep these tasks varied.*

- *Repeat the rules if necessary.*

- *Use short sentences and establish eye contact.*

- *If a student misreads a situation, help them to understand what has happened and give them strategies to use in the future* – in relation to impulsivity, ask them to write down their thoughts and ideas and discuss these later.

- *Utilise behaviour systems* – these need to reflect positive and negative performance.

- *Create boundaries for acceptable and unacceptable behaviour* – make these clear to students and reward/sanction as required.

- *Develop study skills* – for example, typing, use of laptops and calculators.

- *Provide frequent one-to-one feedback and personal contact.*

- *Avoid trying to single out a student with ADHD* – giving them too much attention is not advisable as they will not want to look needy.

- *If students fidget* – give them a stress ball or doodle pad.

- *Give them brain break activities.*

Further reading

O'Regan, F. (2002) *How to Teach and Manage Children with ADHD*. Wisbech: LDA

www.ADDERS.org – run by a parent with a child with ADHD

www.CHADD.org – USA ADHD support group

Oppositional Defiant Disorder (ODD)

Characteristics

Students with ODD will often exhibit the following characteristics:

- Frequent temper tantrums.

- Arguing excessively with adults.

- Active defiance and refusing to comply with adult requests and rules.

- Deliberately annoying people.

- Spite and vindictiveness.

- Seeking revenge.

Treatment/strategies

- *Develop a Behaviour Plan* – when doing this we must remember that the basic drive of a student with ODD is to resist any adult control and manipulation. The more controlling an adult appears to be, the more oppositional a student will become.

- *Create a structured environment* – ODD students need structure, rules, rewards, guidance and a sense of safety. Such an environment will remind them repeatedly of acceptable behaviour limits and expectations.

- *Use behaviour modification techniques* – these should include anger management.

- *Use rewards* – these need to be tangible and given to a student immediately following correct behaviour on their part.

- *Utilise group work* – this may help to enhance students' self-esteem.

- *Remain calm* – try not to show any emotion when reacting to behaviours shown by a student with ODD.

Conduct Disorder (CD)

Characteristics

Conduct Disorder is shown in a repetitive and persistent pattern of behaviour in which the basic rights of others are violated. The following characteristics are based on the *Diagnostic and Statistical Manual of the American Psychiatric Association* (cited in O'Regan, 2002):

- Aggression:

  - bullies, threatens or intimidates others

  - initiates fights

  - uses weapons that could harm others

  - steals from a victim whilst confronting them

- Destruction of property.

- Deceitfulness, lying or stealing.

- Serious violations of rules.

Treatment/strategies

As with ODD, the basic drive of a student with CD is to resist control and manipulation from any adult. The more controlling an adult appears to be, the more oppositional a student will become.

- *Create structure* – use rules, rewards, guidance and a sense of included safety.

- *Model appropriate behaviour* – show what is expected in different situations.

- *Use clear and consistent rewards* – these can help break the cycle of negative behaviour.

- *Provide a person that a student can speak to* – talking through their behaviour with someone is important.

- *Provide therapy* – this may help a student to control different aspects of their behaviour.

- *Reflect on their use of computer games and television* – examining the affect ot these on a student's behaviour can prove very worthwhile.

Further reading

www.aacap.org – American Academy of Child and Adolescent Psychiatry

Tourette Syndrome

Characteristics

The symptoms of Tourette Syndrome can be divided into the following:

- Motor – as a neurological disorder it is characterised by tics which are involuntary, and rapid and sudden movements that occur repeatedly in the same way.

- Vocal – involuntary noises or vocalisations.

- Behavioural – self-destructive behaviours may occur.

Treatment/strategies

- *Most people with Tourette Syndrome do not require medication* – medication can help in severe cases, suppressing tics and making life more manageable. These drugs increase the amount of dophamine in the body but can have side effects.

- *Use behaviour therapies and techniques* – for example, encouraging students to practise a common tic may allow them to have a tic-free episode afterwards (as people with Tourette Syndrome have to make a certain number of tics each day).

- *Help students to adopt exercise and relaxation techniques.*

- *Help students to concentrate on an absorbing task* – this can also prove helpful.

- *Some students seem to be helped by removing additives from their diet* – herbal medicines, vitamin and mineral supplements can also sometimes be of assistance.

- *Be consistent with rewards and sanctions.*

- *Enable students to sit near a door* – this enables them to make an easy exit when necessary because of their condition.

- *Attempt to avoid confrontational situations with students.*

Further reading

www.tourettes-action.org.uk

Reflection on practice

Support strategies to use with students in diverse environments

How would you support a learner with Conduct Disorder and Tourette Syndrome in a classroom and practical area?

Put your responses into the spaces on the grid below.

Table 1.1

	Conduct Disorder	Tourette Syndrome
Support strategies you would use in classroom		
Support strategies you would use in a practical area. Specify area e.g., workshop, salon, catering facility		

How might a Learning Support Assistant (LSA) be used in each area to support those learners?

_____
_____
_____

When might you find time to discuss support strategies with the LSA?

_____
_____
_____

Case Studies

Look at the two Case Studies below. Read through the characteristics of each student's behaviour and try to identify the predominant condition they have, then try to think of any suitable strategies that could be used with them.

Student A

Naseem is a Level 3, 18-year-old student who displays the following behaviours:

- Frequently disrupts the rest of the class.

- Talks continuously and interrupts others.

- Constantly fiddles with objects including his mobile phone.

- Doesn't pay attention and finds it difficult to concentrate.

- Produces very little work.

- Is disrespectful of others.

- Enjoys distracting other students who are trying to work.

- Ignores his lecturers and talks over them when they are trying to teach.

- Is forgetful and loses materials.

Condition

_____

_____

List any strategies you think might be appropriate to use with this learner.

_____

_____

_____

_____

Now check your list with the list of recommended strategies below.

Strategies to use with a learner with ADHD

- Position them in class where they are least likely to be distracted.

- Develop predictable environments, clear rules, boundaries and seating.

- Make the behaviour expectations really clear.

- If they misread a situation help them to understand and give them strategies to use in the future.

- Reward and sanction immediately.

- Intervene early – remind them of rules and consequences.

- Give clear and precise instructions – say their name, maintain firm eye contact, and use short sentences; repeat instructions where necessary; use silence where necessary.

- Give distraction objects to the student to fiddle with e.g. a stress ball.

- Break the session up into clear segments and introduce some oppotunities for physical activity e.g. brain breaks.

Student B

Andy is a 45-year-old student who has recently joined college. He has profound learning and behavioural difficulties. He displays the following behaviours:

- Inflexibility – hates changes to his routine and often finds it difficult to concentrate when this occurs.

- Finds it extremely difficult to adjust to unfamiliar situations.

- When things go wrong he exhibits extreme inappropriate behaviours.

- Has limited use of non-verbal communication – there is a lack of eye contact and facial expressions.

- Uses repetitive language – often his words and phrases are repeated.

- Can be very gifted in certain areas but can also become pre-occupied with certain areas of interest.

- Is reluctant to receive help and support as education was not fully available to him when young and derogatory remarks were made when he was younger about his inability to learn. These have meant that he is very insecure about learning.

Condition

_____

_____

List any strategies you think might be appropriate to use with this learner.

(Continued)

(Continued)

_____

_____

_____

Now check your list with the list of recommended strategies below.

Strategies to use with someone with High Level Autistic Spectrum Disorder

- Develop a structured and predictable environment.

- Focus on their strengths and areas of interest: remember they can be gifted in certain areas; tailor individual learning strategies towards utilising these strengths.

- Build their self-esteem.

- Develop co-operative learning strategies to improve their interactions.

- Ensure they know the overall structure that every lesson will adhere to, e.g. the beginnings and endings will be the same: this will help to avoid any behavioural problems that may arise when they are not able to cope with changes to routine.

- Talk to the learner within the confidentiality conventions to identify any triggers and what you can do to help them with their learning experience.

- Ensure you research the condition.

- Enlist the support of a Learning Support Assistant (LSA) if one is available: team working with an LSA can be of real benefit both to you and the learner.

Key points

- Students will come from a diverse range of backgrounds and have varied prior experiences. This means we need to develop a range of skills to manage the behavioural challenges that may arise.

- More students are arriving with additional needs and statements.

- The causes of challenging behaviour are varied:

  - poor previous learning experiences

  - difficulties in adapting to college life

- home background

- mental health issues

- involvement in crime

- substance abuse

- effects of the media

- effects of food

- Brain re-configuration in adolescence and its effect on learning and behaviour are important. There are many changes to the brain in adolescence that will lead to learners being:

  - impulsive

  - risk taking

  - unable to assess causes and effects

  - less able to assess threats

  - ruled by their emotions

  - unable to recover easily from trauma

  Only when the pre-frontal cortex is fully developed are learners able to plan, set priorities, organise their thoughts, suppress their impulses, and weigh up the consequences of their actions.

- There are a number of issues relating to academic versus vocational groups and teaching combined groups.

- Understanding and supporting additional needs learners involves the following:

  - individual students can suffer from a number of conditions

  - Autism, Asperger Syndrome, ADHD, ODD, CD and Tourette Syndrome have key symptoms/ characteristics and various strategies can be adopted to deal with these

- The challenges of managing students in diverse environments will include practical areas and classrooms.

- Case studies looking at supporting learners with conditions should include older learners with learning and behavioural difficulties.

CHAPTER 2

Making a strong first impression

Making a significant initial impact on students

It is important that you get your first interactions right. The impact that you make during the first few minutes when you meet a group is critical. Imagine each student as a mini bar-code scanner: as they arrive they will zap you, reading your body language and vocal tone. They will assess your hot buttons, what triggers you and makes you angry, what they are likely to get away with. They will throw down various challenges to test you. Often these will occur from several students at once to see how effectively you can manage multiple events. Students are very good at 'testing the water' and finding lecturers' weak points. Many staff will have built up their credibility by proxy – an established reputation will go before them.

Helping students acclimatise to the FE ethos is also key to the induction process. Learners will come from a variety of backgrounds and experiences. Some older students will be returning to learning after a number of years away from formal education; they may well be understandably anxious and need reassurance and support. Some learners will be at college because their employers have insisted they attend in order to improve their vocational qualifications. Learners coming directly from school at 16 or attending college as a 14- to 16-year-old will have a number of reservations as mentioned in Chapter 1. It is vital that we initially try to develop a positive group rapport and help learners to work together in a co-operative manner. We need to develop routines and mutually agreed rules for the mutual benefit of the group. The work we do on this in the establishment phase will be of great benefit to how a group works throughout the year.

In behaviour management terms older learners who are returning to learning for a variety of reasons will need different approaches from those for younger learners. Older learners generally will need lots of support and encouragement to build their self-belief. They will also need lots of support in relation to study skills. However younger learners, and particularly 14- to 16-year-old learners, will come from a variety of settings where the management of their behaviour will have been handled differently. Initially we will need to be quite firm with them in relation to behaviour management. Therefore, to begin with it may be necessary to be a different person from the one you are in the more adult setting of Further Education. Remember not to disclose too much verbally and keep your body language neutral. Also remember to mark your territory. Standing by the door to welcome students is important as it marks out the fact that they are leaving *their* social environment and entering *your* learning environment. It is essential that you deal with any initial challenges effectively. Any weakness or vulnerability on your part will be easily exposed. Giving the right presentation of oneself to students is vital – be firm but friendly and avoid adopting a pleading tone at all costs. It would also be sensible here to have carefully rehearsed your responses beforehand.

Reflection on practice

1   Often learners will arrive directly from school, expect to be spoon-fed, and be unable to work independently. Many will also be lacking in the basic skills of reading and numeracy. What strategies would you employ during induction and in initial sessions to develop their key skills and encourage them to work independently?

_____
_____
_____

2   We will often have to teach groups with a wide range of abilities. We will also be faced with mixed groups containing students on vocational and academic courses. What strategies would you employ to ensure that the work is appropriately differentiated?

_____
_____
_____

Why not try this initially?

- **Greet positioning** – be at the door to meet your group as they arrive: as they enter the room greet them and establish eye contact.

- **Posture** – stand in a confident manner with a straight back and your head looking forward and adopt a relaxed and confident bearing.

- **Vocal tone and command** – when speaking to the students think about your tone and try to have an air of command to your voice. Try to use a strong confident voice and avoid a nervous vocal tone. Practise speaking at the lower end of your two-octave vocal cord range. When nervous we tend to speak at the higher end in a squeaky voice which indicates a lack of confidence.

- **Power position** – when speaking to the whole group stand in a position where you can scan or 'lighthouse' the whole group. Position yourself in the classroom so that you have a wide field of vision. Try not to position yourself so that students are behind you. Scan the room repeatedly. Aim to make eye contact with as many of the group as possible. Remember that some challenging and poorly behaved students try to gravitate towards your 'blind spot' just in front of you.

- **Silence** – use of silence can be very effective. For example Clint Eastwood used this to great effect in the 'Dollar' series of movies and created a 'person of mystery'.

- **Patrolling** – remember to patrol the whole of the classroom and mark your territory. Remain mobile and move around while mingling with the students – no-go areas should not exist.

- **Proximity** – moving towards and standing alongside students who are not working, slightly within their 46cm personal space bubble, can be a powerful tool.

- **Level** – standing over a student who is not working can put you at a psychological advantage. However, doing so can also be intimidating so this should be used infrequently. When discussing points with a student it is best to sit or crouch at a slightly lower level alongside them. This will make communication more effective and reduce the likelihood of any conflict if your discussion relates to behaviour matters.

- **Positioning** – when students are working it can sometimes be an effective strategy to stand at the back of the classroom.

- **Gaze** – use firm eye contact and focus on eye-to-eye contact. Keep this contact between the eyes and at a point on the centre of the subject's forehead. Avoid eye dips which can be seen as being submissive and eye shuttle where you flick your eyes back and forth. Kuhnke (2007: 77–79) states that in order to build rapport we need to meet the other person's gaze for 60 to 70 per cent of the time. She also suggests, however, that the average mutual gaze only lasts 1.8 seconds and goes on to describe how Bill Clinton could make an individual feel important and valued by using his eyes to engage his listener and by letting his gaze scan across their eyes and face as he spoke. (A word of caution is necessary here: remember that prolonged eye contact in some cultures can be seen as being discourteous.) You will get a clearer indication of how responsive a person is by looking at the size of their pupils. In normal light conditions if the pupils are dilated (wide) then the person is relaxed and positive. However if the pupils are narrow, then the opposite is true and we may need to be wary.

- **Facial expressions** – we can give away a lot of information by the facial expressions we adopt and so we must think carefully about these (more information on this is contained in Chapter 5, 'The Importance of Body Language').

- **Seating plan** – ensure that you allocate seats to students and have a seating plan. Having named photographs is good for this as there is nothing more powerful than calling out a student's name when they are about to engage in some poor behaviour. If younger students choose to change places use a stopwatch to time the length of the disruption whilst they return to their normal places and then detain them later for an appropriate length of time.

- **Be 'manically' vigilant** – in the first few sessions make sure each transgression or example of poor behaviour is dealt with firmly.

- **Anticipation** – in the first few sessions try to anticipate when poor behaviour is likely to occur and intervene straight away. Dealing with incidents immediately stops them from escalating: 'The time to repair the roof is when the sun is shining' (John F. Kennedy, State of the Union Address, 1 November 1962).

It is essential that you are well organised and prepared and can create a firm yet confident image. The 'don't smile 'til Christmas' maxim may be useful, and it is certainly easier to loosen the reins than it is to tighten them, but even more powerful in this instance can be smiling in a relaxed, confident way.

The importance of establishing rules, routines and protocols

- Establish mutually agreed rules in the first session. Clear boundaries need to be established and expectations regarding behaviour must be made clear. In practical areas there will also be a need to outline these in relation to key Health and Safety issues.

- Agree the protocols for different types of work and for the beginnings and ends of sessions. Establish a 'take-up time' at the start of each lesson – such as allowing two minutes for learners to settle. If students take longer, use a stopwatch to check the duration of any time wasting and detain the relevant individuals at the end of the session for that period of time. It would be helpful to have a take-up activity in place on the whiteboard for students to do at the start.

- At the beginning of each session explain the work that will be covered and the learning that will take place. This should be linked with the work covered in the previous session, showing how it fits into the bigger picture.

- Agree on how the transitions will take place between different types of work.

- Make any instructions clear and differentiate the work so all learners can achieve.

- Have a strategy for settling the group at the end of the session and for students' orderly exit. Bringing learning together in plenary and issuing rewards earned during the session are good strategies to use.

- Rules should be established co-operatively with students. These should be:

  ○ few, clear and simple

  ○ collaboratively constructed

  ○ described positively and reinforced by rewarding good behaviour: reward all those students who behave well

  ○ understood by everyone and the reasons for them clearly explained

  ○ agreed and consistently applied by all.

Routines

Creating and then maintaining clear and predictable routines that are appropriate to your teaching area is an essential task:

- During the establishment phase, at the beginning of the year, time needs to be invested in establishing your routines – this will save you time later in the year.

- Halfway through the first term these routines will need reinforcing during the Consolidation Phase – as Bill Rogers (2004: 5.2) says, 'effective teachers always maintain, consolidate and "habituate" what they establish … a progressive "habituation" regarding behaviour and learners'.

- Clear expectations regarding behaviour that are supported by clear consequences are a necessity.

Lesson rules and routines

Start of the lesson

- Be punctual arriving at lessons (lecturers should be there before students).

- Establish clear routines to settle students and to show a preparedness for the lesson. Set a target time in which students should be seated, having removed their outdoor clothes, got out any materials, and put their bags on the floor.

- Try to avoid unnecessary queuing in corridors and receive students in an orderly fashion.

- Discourage interruptions or queries until you have got the whole class working.

- Establish a clear signal that the lesson has started – for example, using a countdown, clicking your fingers.

- Begin the lesson only when all students are quiet and paying attention.

- Ensure you have a crisp and stimulating start to your lesson.

During the lesson

- Stay in control and vigilant throughout the lesson.

- Plan and organise the classroom and the lesson around keeping students interested to minimise any opportunity for disruptions to occur.

- Have a series of non-verbal cues and positive attention getters to enable students to come back together at key points in the lesson. It is good to establish a learning ritual for this where you will give learners a 'one-minute-to-go' cue that will quickly get the class back together.

- Ensure tasks are clearly explained and supported in a written form.

- Develop your ability to handle simultaneous events – selectively ignoring some behaviours may be appropriate here.

End of the lesson

- Conclude with a summary of what has been learnt and give a brief overview of the content of the next lesson.

- How we dismiss students at the end of a lesson is significant: be positive, issue any rewards, thank them for their work, and say that you are looking forward to working with them in the next lesson.

Spatial anchoring

Non-verbal communication extends beyond tics, tells and body posture. Think about where you stand for different purposes in your learning environment. We all use spatial anchoring or spotlight states in our teaching. Imagine the classroom as a theatrical stage with spotlights set up to highlight certain areas where actors will congregate at different times in the play. You can then choose various spotlight areas that are suitable for your particular purpose and stand in these in order to evoke a specific response from learners.

Reflection on practice

With a partner think about where you stand in your learning environment for these actions:

- The greeting position

- Imparting information

- A questioning position

- Bringing a group together after an activity

- Reinforcing rules

- A sanctioning position

- A relaxed calming position

- Plenary time

- Position to indicate the end of a session/exit time.

By standing in these positions without saying anything your students will have a clearer indication of what is about to happen and this can make transitions or interactions easier.

Try to develop a routine where you can use spatial anchoring for successfully managing student behaviour.

Managing initial challenges

We said at the beginning of this chapter that students will initially be assessing both you and your ability to manage their behaviour and that your responses to those initial challenges will set the behavioural climate in your classroom for the course's duration. It is essential that you select the key behavioural issues you will have to challenge first and to perhaps do this by choosing to tactically ignore some less significant behaviours and deal with those later on.

When challenging a student about their inappropriate behaviour it is important that you:

- do not over verbalise and that you are specific in your language

- place yourself in their eyeline

- clearly state the inappropriate behaviour you wish to discuss (thereby separating the behaviour from the student)

- speak calmly and maintain eye contact if they dispute the issue. Use 'the broken record technique' which is to repeat the behaviour you wish to discuss

- emphasise that they own the behaviour and it is their choice as to whether or not they continue with this behaviour or choose another course. To help them with this refer to the college's Code of Conduct and any consequence that will occur if they continue with their inappropriate behaviour. This then de-personalises the issue

- are aware that when some students are challenged about their poor behaviour they will try to divert your attention from the primary behaviour by smoke screening or adopting a distracting secondary behaviour. This can be done by sulking, looking away from you, and making all manner of gestures. If they are caught doing something they may well deny the fact or say that the person next to them had started it. They may also suggest that you are always picking on them, or that you let others get away with it, or that another colleague lets them do it. In these circumstances tactically ignore the behaviour – avoid arguing and focus on the primary behaviour. Block out their comments and do not respond to them. Use the broken record technique above of repeating the same line – 'I am referring to you and [xxx behaviour]'. If you can do this in a commanding voice this may prove to be a powerful tool

- ignore other students if they join in and support the student. Blank out their comments and do not let them become involved. If necessary move to another location with the student

- in certain situations take a Time Out, thereby allowing the student some time to reflect. This can often take the heat out of the situation. (Strategies for dealing with a range of challenging behaviours will be given in Chapter 8.)

Reflection on practice

Weekly Behaviour Management Log

Keep your own Behaviour Management Log for the first half-term. Try to add your repertoire of approaches over the duration of the log. To gain ideas, talk to a colleague or use some strategies given in this book.

Date	Subject	Session	Score: how lesson went in behaviour management terms (1 = Poor, 5 = Good)	Strategies that worked	Strategies that didn't work	Next lesson I will try ... (Discuss with a colleague)

Photocopiable: *How to Manage Behaviour in Further Education* (Second Edition)
© David Vizard 2012

Case Studies A and B

In pairs discuss how you might manage the following.

Case Study A

One older male learner in a group is particularly challenging to a younger female lecturer in her first year of teaching. He:

- is quite confrontational and questions the authority, knowledge and experience of the lecturer

- identifies an area of weakness in the lecturer's knowledge and continually asks questions in that area in order to undermine her

- quietly makes sarcastic comments about the lecturer to other students whilst she is teaching

- does everything he can to undermine her

- has been forced to attend the course by his employer to gain extra qualifications for a job he has been doing for years.

If you were this lecturer what kinds of strategies would you use with this learner to get them onside?

1 _____
_____

2 _____
_____

3 _____
_____

4 _____
_____

5 _____
_____

Compare your strategies with your partner.

Discuss your strategies with another group.

Some strategies/points to consider in relation to Case Study A

Get behind the reason for this behaviour:

- Are they being encouraged by their employer to gain an extra qualification for the job they are already doing and in fact don't believe they need this? It is important to sell the benefits of the course to them.

- Are they feeling vulnerable by returning to an educational setting – are they afraid of feeling stupid or that they won't be able to do the work? Reassurance and encouragement needs to be given to them. Attempt to build their self-confidence. Use a buddy in the group to support them.

- Address the issue of their poor attitude towards you. Show you have a lot of experience and relevant knowledge. Build up your credibility in their eyes.

- If their negativity continues liaise closely with their employer – they would not be happy with a member of staff who was representing their firm displaying such a negative attitude.

- Use the behaviour management strategies given in this chapter to build rapport with the learner and make a strong start by challenging and managing the inappropriate behaviour straight away.

Case Study B

A group of vocational students are difficult to keep on board due to their having a low boredom threshold. They are hard to motivate and expect a much faster-paced environment. Many also have issues because they do not want to be there as they feel they can already do the job without the qualification the course offers. Because of this reluctance and resistance they are turning up late, attempting to leave early, and displaying their dissatisfaction by yawning loudly throughout the lesson, chatting loudly with others, or continually using their mobile phones. They are also using inappropriate language in college by swearing and adopting racist or homophobic terms. Depending on their work environment some students seem oblivious to the fact that such comments are not acceptable. What would you need to do to deal with this group effectively?

1 _____
_____

2 _____
_____

3 _____
_____

4 _____
_____

5 _____
_____

Compare your strategies with your partner.

What is your College Policy relating to racist and homophobic comments?

Some strategies/points to consider in relation to Case Study B

- It is essential to be firm establishing clear ground rules relating to behaviour and refer to the Code of Conduct.

- Emphasise that you will be linking up with their employer regularly and feeding back on their progress.

(Continued)

(Continued)

- Clearly outline the policy relating to diversity issues, bullying and appropriate language use during the induction process. Make it clear that swearing and using racist and homophobic terms will not be tolerated and significant action will be taken if these are used in relation to College Policy and legal requirements.

- Use the strategies relating to lateness, use of mobiles and other inappropriate behaviours given elsewhere in the book. Be extremely vigilant initially and respond to any challenges.

- Make it a clear expectation that you will have a plenary session at the end of each lesson in which all learners must take part.

- Develop co-operative approaches to learning where students are responsible for their learning and that of group members.

- Emphasise strongly to learners the benefits of completing the course.

- Develop a rewards system that gives instant gratification for the successful completion of work.

Key points

- It is essential to get initial interactions with the group right.

- Thorough induction procedures which take into account learners' variety of backgrounds and experiences need to be in place in order to acclimatise students to an FE ethos.

- To identify the different approaches needed to support learners you will have to remember that:

  - there will be learners coming directly from school who will need help to develop their independent learning skills

  - an appropriate differentiation will be required for mixed groups containing vocational and academic course students

- Making an initial impact on learners when they enter the classroom is important because this represents a defining moment.

- Students will be reading you from the very first moment so you will need to be aware of your body language, your vocal tone, and the scripts you use – learners will make their initial assumptions very quickly so giving the right presentation of yourself is essential.

- You should meet and greet students as they arrive.

- Tactically pausing and using silence (in a 3–5 second gap) is a very powerful tool.

- Positioning is vital – note the importance of spatial anchoring.

- You must be aware of eye contact, vocal tone, and your use of cues – all of these are key tools in the classroom.

- You can manage initial challenges well by using the broken record technique and ignoring smoke-screening and secondary behaviours.

- Older students who offer challenges to younger staff must be managed in a firm way.

- Dis-engaged vocational students should be kept engaged by using appropriate activities.

CHAPTER 3

Creating positive learning environments

The importance of developing positive learning environments

Some students will only have experienced negativity in many aspects of their lives and as a result will offer high levels of challenge and extreme behaviour. They will soon find it is easier to gain negative attention by misbehaving rather than attention for positive reasons. When faced with such groups of students it is extremely difficult to envisage creating a positive learning environment in which they can work. However, remember that creating a positive learning environment will have a powerful impact on learner behaviour. We must not underestimate the influence we can have in our learning environments. Tyrer (2004: 19) cites Ginnott (1972) who made this clear when describing the work of a teacher: 'I am the decisive element in the classroom. It is my personal approach that creates the climate'. Buscaglia, cited by Vizard (2009: 45), has also described the power of being positive: 'Fantastic things happen to the way we feel, to the way we make people feel. All this simply by using positive words'. We need to use praise, when warranted, in a ratio of at least five praise statements to one negative statement. Praise those students in a group who arrive punctually and bring the necessary equipment/materials with them. Over a period of time learners will discover it is more likely that they will gain your attention through adopting positive behaviour than by using negative behaviour.

How positive learning environments can be developed by the use of verbal and non-verbal communication

The following strategies will help:

- Give out nuggets of praise to learners when these are warranted – catch students when they are being good. To help improve their self-esteem we also ought to regularly give out 'emotional small change' to learners in the form of praise. It is worthwhile remembering that we can never give enough praise.

- The way we greet students on arrival can have an influence on whether or not our learning environment will have a positive ethos. Standing by the door engaging in eye contact as they arrive and talking to them, using first names, and relating to their interests are all essential: this gives students the message that you are interested in them as individuals.

- We need to establish a variety of routines, such as a two-minute take-up time on arrival to allow students to settle. Introducing a take-up activity at the beginning will assist learners with tuning into the session. This helps to create a positive atmosphere and focuses their attention. (Note that a range of useful websites listing free starter activity resources is given in the appendices.)

- When speaking to students you should be calm and use a pleasant tone. Using appropriate humour is also important if this is backed up with a smile – it can help to lighten the atmosphere.

- In disciplinary interventions you need to be assertive rather than aggressive. It is important to keep your own and students' dignity intact.

- Acknowledge those students who are getting it right. Always praise positive behaviour by naming the behaviour back to a student. Remember also that courtesy is contagious.

- When giving instructions to students or making requests it is vital to be polite but not pleading.

- Being aware of spatial anchoring or 'psychological geography' in our learning environment is important (see the reference to this in Chapter 2). We will stand in certain positions for particular actions: for example, we will have a point in the room where we will stand in order to control the group and sanction them – this is the 'discipline position'. We will also have a position where we will sit for informal/relaxed conversations and we will have a position we stand in when we are imparting knowledge. We may also have a variety of locations when we move around the room from which we praise students – for example, often making use of our proximity and level, and usually crouching to one side of a student. Remember that at the end of a session it is worthwhile having a relaxed ending – thank learners for their input and say that you look forward to working with them at the next session.

- Body language, in the form of non-verbal communication, can have a significant influence on the type of atmosphere we create. Sometimes if you approach a badly behaving group with trepidation and fear this will show in your body language and vocal tone. Try to work on your body language to make sure this does not happen.

- Sometimes using positive affirmations or statements can help: for example – 'This group may be challenging but I will gain experience from doing this'.

- Sometimes lecturers will sub-consciously adopt barrier gestures when they have to face groups that are poorly behaved. These gestures include:

  ○ folding their arms across the chest

  ○ standing behind a physical barrier such as a table

- clutching papers or books in their arms

- exhibiting nervous tics or tells that show a lack of confidence – increased blinking, rubbing their neck or nose, varying their vocal tone, excessively shuffling their feet or making leg movements, or excessively clearing their throat.

This can be helped by instead adopting a relaxed position. This can be achieved by:

- using open palm gestures

- allowing the arms to be open – creating a more confident bearing

- asymmetrically positioning the limbs

- giving a sideways lean and tilt to the head.

- To create a positive environment non-verbally, you need to develop positive eye contact and friendly facial expressions and use positive non-verbal communication, such as giving a thumbs-up gesture to show your agreement/pleasure. Smiling and nodding your head can also show active listening.

- By making effective use of silence you can give students time to formulate their answers following your asking a question. If they do make an error in their response help them to correct this by signposting the answer by using cues. In addition, to develop rapport with a student non-verbally remember that on some occasions it can be appropriate to mirror their body language.

Reflection on practice

Think about five different ways in which you create a positive learning environment both verbally and non-verbally.

Verbally

1 _____
_____

2 _____
_____

3 _____
_____

4 _____
_____

5 _____
_____

Non-verbally

1 _____
_____

2 _____
_____

3 _____
_____

4 _____
_____

5 _____
_____

Here are some examples to help you.

Verbally

- Use students' first names.

- Be interactive with students.

- Listen to them.

- Use humour.

- Praise good behaviour and work.

Non-verbally

- Smile.

- Use an open stance.

- Make eye contact.

- Nod in response when a student speaks.

- Use privately understood signals.

The 10 Rs of positive behaviour management

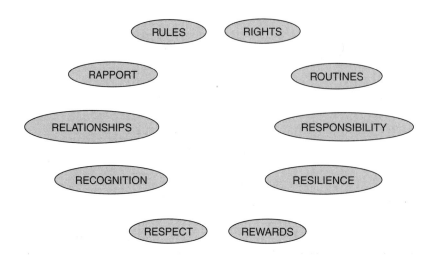

Figure 3.1   The 10 Rs of positive behaviour management

These are the 10 elements that are fundamental when developing a positive system of behaviour management. In the previous chapter we discussed the importance of setting up clear, mutually agreed rules and routines in the establishment phase at the beginning of the year which will take into account students' rights. The other seven Rs are listed below.

Recognition

It is important to recognise the individual differences and interests of our students. By chatting to them informally we can learn a lot about individuals. (Think how empowering it is to us when a line manager remembers a fact about us outside college and chats to us about it.)

Rapport

Recognising those differences is the first step in establishing rapport with our students. Mirroring students' body language is another good way to develop this rapport. Just watch car or double glazing salespeople in action – they use body language mirroring to help develop a link with customers. Listening to speech patterns and adopting students' rate of speech and using similar sentence lengths and vocal rhythms are all helpful.

In addition, when a student is upset or angry listen carefully to the words they use when they speak. When learners are upset they will tend to use words relating to their sensory preferences: for example, they may say 'I feel very upset' (kinaesthetic preference) or 'I can't see the point' (visual preference). If we talk back to them framing our words in the language of their sensory preference we will be more able to connect with them and move them on from an agitated state to a calmer one more quickly.

Respect

Respect is another key element to building a positive climate; if students respect a member of staff then they are less likely to pose behaviour problems for them. If mutually respectful exchanges take place between all members of the community then there is more chance of a positive ethos existing. In such communities staff will:

- listen to students

- care about their opinions

- not give up on them

- help them and take the time to explain things

- make students feel special and clever

- enjoy students' company and be keen and enthusiastic about their subject

- diffuse difficult situations by allowing students to save face and avoid confrontation

- model good behaviour.

Always remember that it is easy to humiliate a young person but much harder to build up their self-esteem.

Relationships

Try to remember that students who are most in need of positive relationships are also the ones who are more used to failing than succeeding. Relationships are a vital part of developing a positive climate. There is also a real difference between relationships and interactions. In many settings interactions will take place but the relationships between staff and students will be poor. In those where relationships are good, staff will:

- learn students' names and use them

- give positive greetings – welcoming students at the beginning of sessions and saying farewell at the end

- remember details of their individuality

- be fair and consistent

- be patient and have a sense of humour

- be respectful and care for students

- find time to listen to them even when they are busy

- make students feel safe and secure in class

- make allowances for students when they are having a bad day

- show mutual respect (a relationship will break down if a student believes that a member of staff does not like them)

- set firm but fair boundaries.

Responsibility

Giving responsibility to students is perhaps one of the most difficult things to achieve. It is important to remember that responsibility grows with responsibilities, so give students responsibilities and choices: 14- to16-year-olds in college settings will talk enthusiastically and positively about their experiences and the responsibility they have been given. One student described their experiences to me as a 'boost in life'. Seeing learners in Hospitality and Catering serving food to staff, students and members of the public, or students working with members of the public in Hair and Beauty, is always a positive experience as students thrive on the extra responsibilities this work brings. It does this by increasing their involvement and generating a sense of ownership. In Chapter 1 we looked at the positive effects of giving real responsibility to young adults in other societies leading to an earlier maturation of the frontal lobes of the brain: this has been shown to have a positive impact on their behaviour and the ability to study. So it is essential we give students every opportunity to assume some real responsibilities in our learning environments.

Reflection on practice

1   In groups of five generate a thought shower of the best practice you can see in a learning environment where real responsibilities are given to learners. One group member should record comments on a sheet of flipchart paper.

2   From these, list the best five ideas generated.

Resilience

Many young people whose behaviour is challenging have extremely low levels of self-esteem. This is probably because they have had very bad experiences within education and the testing system has further reinforced their negative self-image. As a result it is vital to try to build on that level of self-esteem and increase learners' resilience.

Learners with low self-esteem display the following characteristics:

- have a negative self-image

- take few risks

- have limited communication skills

- feel that they have no control over their lives.

We can build on their self-esteem level by adopting the strategies outlined in this chapter. Frieman (2001) has found that resilient students:

- are problem solvers

- can gain the positive attention of others

- have an optimistic view of life

- feel independent

- approach life from a proactive perspective

- feel that they have control over their environment

- have a sense of humour

- can empathise with others

- have effective problem-solving skills and coping strategies.

Always remember that it is not difficult to humiliate a young person but much harder to build up their self-esteem. Benjamin Disraeli demonstrated the important role of building self-esteem: 'The greatest good you can do for another is not just to share your riches but to reveal to him his own'.

Rewards

In developing a positive learning environment great care should be taken to ensure an appropriate system of rewards is in place. If praise is regularly given rather than the lecturer giving undue attention to negative behaviour, then the former will be seen as the best way to get a member of staff's attention.

A renowned myth that exists in many colleges is that older students do not like rewards and will have no desire to take part in reward schemes. In discussions with various students I have found the opposite to be true: that learners of all ages want to be involved in reward schemes. Involving students in developing suitable systems for this is important as it helps to give them ownership of whatever scheme is taken up – for example, by designing stickers and certificates.

One of the best ways to reward students is not by using a tangible form but by giving out 'verbal reinforcers' and 'nuggets of praise', or adopting non-verbal reinforcers such as friendly facial expressions, positive eye contact, and other gestures.

How to create stimulating and positive learning environments

In order to create a positive learning environment our teaching areas need to be stimulating and interesting places. However, the reality is that we may have to teach in a large number of rooms and have little control over our environment. We may also have to teach in workshops and practical areas that will place restrictions on what we can and cannot do. I believe it is important for us to have as much ownership of our spaces as possible by negotiating with other colleagues who use those same spaces.

Case Study A

I recently visited one Leisure and Tourism room in a college in south-west England which was a virtual visual feast. Inflatable sharks and dolphins were suspended from the ceiling together with an inflatable globe. Lots of bright visual materials were dotted around the walls. Potted plants were in one corner and a poster for a feature film was hung on the wall beside it, with the main character expounding the values of Geography in speech bubbles (added to the poster by the lecturer).

With over 90 per cent of student learning being unconscious it is vital that we make their surroundings visually stimulating. We must be aware, however, that too much in the way of a display, particularly if this is poorly arranged, can lead to visual clutter, which can in turn have a negative impact (particularly on those students with conditions such as ADHD).

Case Study B

Many rooms will have word walls and word mobiles of key terminology. I have seen A3 word mats used successfully in a number of areas. In one Sport and Leisure session a member of staff was using these with students. The session was dealing with muscle groups and the mats had a diagram of all of the muscles in the human body and the key words that were associated with these groups. Students were able to highlight on the mats the various muscle groups that were used when exercising.

I have also seen these mats used as place mats onto which students can place their work, with key terminology and information visible around the edge of the work as an *aide-mémoire*. In addition, many rooms will have key information on how to approach activities and information on the learning cycle.

Other examples of good practice are given below.

Case Study C

Playing music can be uplifting and also boost learners' performance and intelligence for short periods of time. Music that has 60 or less beats per minute can also have a de-stressing effect. (One example of this is the theme for the feature film *Elvira Madigan*, which uses a Mozart piece (Piano Concerto No. 21) that has proven highly effective. Students have shown a drop in blood pressure and pulse rate when listening to it.) When such music is played the co-ordination centre of the brain is stimulated, endorphins are released, and blood pressure is lowered. This will lead to decreasing levels of adrenalin in students and they will be calmer and less likely to be aggressive. Other types of music can be used with faster beats that are uplifting and motivating.

One lecturer I recently observed used a set piece of music five to 10 minutes in length when he wanted students to work quietly and independently. From an early stage his students had been preconditioned so that when they heard this piece of music they knew that they were required to work quietly.

Reflection on practice

1   With a partner discuss the ways in which you can create a stimulating learning environment in your teaching area.

_____

_____

_____

2   What are the challenges relating to developing positive learning environments, particularly in relation to peripheral learning in workshops and practical areas?

_____

_____

_____

Some points to consider in relation to the activity:

In many practical areas there will be a large number of Health and Safety factors to consider and this can have an impact on work. Often peripheral learning notices may be restricted and in some areas not allowed. Also a range of staff may have use of the workshops and practical areas, so ownership of a space may be a challenge. There is generally little to no flexibility in moving equipment and altering workspaces because many of these are fixed. Many areas also have to have strict rules relating to the use of certain items – for example, hot pans, ovens, ramps, jacks, guillotines and blowtorches.

There is another challenge here as well because many learners can find it difficult to conform to the specialist protective clothing and items they have to wear. Examples of these include eye and ear protectors and protective clothing that can include hard capped boots and hair coverings. An additional impediment can be students having to provide the right equipment/tools. We need to build as positive a learning environment as we can using many of the strategies given above. Working in classrooms for theory/portfolio work can allow you to fully implement such strategies.

3   Complete the positive behaviour management questionnaire given below in relation to your learning environment. Answer questions 1–10 with Yes or No and score statements 11–20 on a scale of 1–5, with 1 indicating 'strongly disagree' and 5 'strongly agree'.

If you have six or more Yes responses to statements 1–10, and your total score for statements 11–20 is 40 or more, then you have a positive learning environment. If you have six or more No responses to statements 1–10, and a total score of 20 or less to statements 11–20, then you may need to reflect on your practice.

Positive Behaviour Management Questionnaire

Circle YES or NO to these statements:

1 Students receive appropriate verbal praise. YES/NO

2 I use good non-verbal communication to promote positive relationships. YES/NO

3 I always keep an accurate record of rewards issued to students. YES/NO

4 I try to encourage an environment where success is celebrated. YES/NO

5 A strategy I use is to preface a correctional statement with a positive comment. YES/NO

6 Students are praised for good behaviour. YES/NO

7 I always try to give some positive comments on written feedback. YES/NO

8 Smiling staff and students are frequently seen in college. YES/NO

9 Peripheral learning notices accentuate the positive. YES/NO

10 The student reward system is balanced, recognising academic, non-academic, extra-curricular activities and service to the community. YES/NO

TOTAL NUMBER OF YES RESPONSES TO STATEMENTS 1–10 ......

Circle 1, 2, 3, 4 or 5 where 1 = STRONGLY DISAGREE and 5 = STRONGLY AGREE:

11 All students' contributions are valued. 1 2 3 4 5

12 The reward system is clear to all staff and students. 1 2 3 4 5

13 Students were involved in the development of the system of rewards. 1 2 3 4 5

14 Students appear relaxed and motivated in all lessons. 1 2 3 4 5

15 Positive comments by the lecturer outweigh negative comments. 1 2 3 4 5

16 High quality work results in the college always recognising this achievement. 1 2 3 4 5

17 There are enough levels in the reward system to reward high achieving students. 1 2 3 4 5

18 Rewards issued are relevant and appreciated by the target age group. 1 2 3 4 5

19 Group rewards are beneficial and help improve motivation. 1 2 3 4 5

20 When correcting a student for poor behaviour I explain why the behaviour is inappropriate. 1 2 3 4 5

TOTAL SCORE FOR RESPONSES TO STATEMENTS 11–20 ......

Photocopiable: *How to Manage Behaviour in Further Education* (Second Edition)
© David Vizard 2012

Case studies of reward systems that actually work

Success is the lifeblood of us all – when we are successful and receive praise it makes us feel really good. Success gives a feeling of achievement and inspires students to attain higher goals. It makes them feel good about themselves and raises their confidence.

The best reward systems are those in which students have an input into their development. In some colleges students have helped in the design of certificates, reward cards and stickers. This in turn gives them ownership of the scheme.

It is also important that all sections, divisions, subject areas and staff in the institution are involved in the application of these rewards.

Some schemes/systems that work include the following:

- Reward systems at their simplest level can be a recognition of a student's achievement – a record of their progress and acquisition of key skills in a subject. In one Hair and Beauty area students asked the lecturer to produce a wallchart on which stickers were placed as students acquired skills.

- In another location students were given pin badges with symbols of their subject as rewards. Many students wore these with pride. They had been sponsored by a local badge-making firm with which the college had links.

- In other colleges I have seen reward certificates/cards issued which were a little different. These were issued at three levels: Bronze, Silver and Gold. To make them different the Bronze Award was postcard size, the Silver Award was half-postcard size, and the Gold Award was postage stamp size. Each had a different cartoon illustration, positive statements, and the level achieved on them. To add another dimension they had been made collectable by having Trump card facts on the reverse. So, for example, at each level there would be different collectable cards on a theme, either football teams, or music, or food, or films. This made them well sought-after items.

- Group rewards can be really motivational. In one catering area the chef used a large pasta jar with lines drawn on it. The lines represented different levels of reward. When individual students or the group did good work a fistful of pasta was added to the jar. If there was a problem pasta was removed. Thus the level could fluctuate. At the end of the week/month the level would be checked and any rewards would be issued to all members of the group. The group would often modify the behaviour of those students who would occasionally overstep the mark.

- Many colleges will have a range of amenities that students can enjoy as a part of a reward system. An example of this includes free beauty treatments, a free hair make-over, and free meals in college restaurants.

- In some locations I have seen lecturers issue Teaching and Learning banknotes of varying unitary value. These would be issued when students completed key components of modules. These notes could then be exchanged for reward items such as stationery items, including pens from the college shop.

- Putting fluorescent card stars into a box with a student's name on as a reward is another system I have seen in use. At the end of a given period the stars are counted up and the student with the most stars gains a reward. These rewards could be issued to all students with stars in the box, at varying levels depending on the number of stars they had gained.

- A Building and Construction lecturer in one college uses Golden Time with his learners. As components of a session are completed students build up units of Golden Time.

These can then be cashed in later. In this context the units count towards time in the sports hall playing lunchtime soccer which he referees.

- In a number of E2E schemes (Entry to Employment) students who have re-engaged with education are rewarded for completing various sections of their modules: on completion of 50 per cent of a module a CD voucher is issued; completing 75 per cent of a module equals cinema tickets being given; and for completing 100 per cent of a module a total of £35 in cash is awarded.

- Many colleges have 'Student of the Week' in different subject areas. The learner's photo is displayed and, as is the case in many jobs, a badge is worn. Achievements and rewards are also recognised in newsletters. For many students the appreciation shown by lecturers and peers is important.

- Some colleges hold termly award ceremonies where students receive a variety of awards for their work.

- Other colleges, to celebrate rights of passage, will generate Year Books or CDs/DVDS of all student achievements in a photographic/video form.

Key points

- Create a positive learning environment which will have a significant impact on student behaviour.

- Try to make positive statements in a proportion of five positive to one negative statement.

- Give out 'emotional small change' to learners to boost their self-esteem.

- Meet and greet students as they arrive for the session.

- Establish rules and routines early on.

- Be polite but not pleading.

- Make verbal reinforcers positive by using students' first names.

- Remember that body language and vocal tone/command account for over 90 per cent of communication.

- Use open not closed body language and assume a relaxed position.

- Be aware of your psychological geography/spatial anchoring.

- Use positive non-verbal cues.

- Make effective use of silence.

- Remember the 10 Rs of positive behaviour management.

- Create a stimulating learning environment.

- Develop a range of positive learning notices and strategies in practical areas and workshops after considering any important Health and Safety issues.

- Conduct an audit of your learning environment to indicate key areas of success and those in need of development.

- Develop a range of rewards for learners and remember the importance of how we create a positive learning environment both verbally and non-verbally.

CHAPTER 4

Effective strategies to use with students displaying challenging behaviour

Seven useful Ps to use when managing inappropriate behaviour

Postures

The posture you adopt can have a significant impact on your voice. To develop an appropriate vocal delivery:

- Be relaxed, an upright posture will help project your voice. If you are slumped, your voice could sound strained. Use body language that conveys authority.

- Control your breathing. Efficient breathing is important in voice control.

- Speak slowly and clearly. Avoid slurring/losing the endings of words. Articulating sounds will help you sound more decisive and authoritative.

- Try to vary your volume to match the circumstances.

The body postures we adopt can also have an effect on our ability to manage challenging behaviour successfully. Churches and Terry (2007: 63–67), in describing the work of Virginia Satir, state that we use one or more of the six communication styles. These are:

- Blaming – postures involve finger stabbing and non-fluid gestures. These can be seen as aggressive, lead to disagreements, and suggest faults in those listening.

- Placating – a non-assertive posture and position where a person seeks sympathy and will accept the blame for most things. This posture should be avoided at all costs with challenging groups as learners will think this shows a significant sign of weakness. However, this position should be used on a one-to-one basis when giving difficult feedback.

- Computing – a posture that hides emotions and suggests detachment, showing no indication of real views or feelings. This body posture illustrates someone who is removed or disassociated.

- Distracting – this posture will use a variety of positions to remove attention from oneself. In language this involves generalising and people will feel someone is not making sense.

- Levelling – this body posture is balanced with the palms facing downwards. This can have a calming effect and give an indication that someone is being truthful. It is also an influential posture.

- Sequencing – a posture that uses measured, controlled movements from the side to the centre of the body. This can make someone appear to be lacking in emotion but thoughtful. The body posture and language used can make someone seem like a computer.

Reflection on practice

In groups of four reflect on which postures you might wish to adopt in a learning environment in the following situations:

1   Giving feedback to an individual student who has just failed a major course assignment.

   _____
   _____
   _____

2   With a group of very demanding Uniform Public Services students – who only respond to the very strict and authoritarian approach of certain lecturers with a military background.

   _____
   _____
   _____

3   You have a rather challenging and unhelpful work-based learning provider. Which postures might you adopt in a meeting with them following an incident of poor behaviour from one of your students?

   _____
   _____
   _____

4   Is there a need to develop flexibility in the communication styles we use, e.g. adopting different postures in various settings?

   _____
   _____
   _____

Pitch and tone

- Most of us have a pitch range of about two octaves, with men's pitch range lower than women's because of their vocal chord length.

- People make assumptions about a person from the pitch of their voice. A low-pitched voice can give the impression of control and authority, whereas a high-pitched voice may appear emotional or a soft target for misbehaving students.

- Be assertive not aggressive. Practise making your voice sound more commanding, decisive, strong and authoritative. It is vital to adopt a confident tone with students.

- Make your point by varying the tone of your voice. Be aware of the situation and remember that sometimes a calming tone may be the best option. Try to keep in mind 'calm words, calm children'.

- Vary your volume to match the specific circumstance.

- Avoid using a pleading tone.

Pacing

- Remember to pace and pause.

- On average we use about 125 words per minute when speaking in public. Speaking quicker than this may give the impression of being too nervous.

- Varying the pace can help us to communicate more effectively and keep students' attention. However, try to avoid speaking too much and too quickly and thus keep your message short and simple.

Vizard (2009: 29) suggests that pacing 'is about really listening to a person and understanding where they are coming from. Whilst pacing you build rapport by picking up and matching their body language, behaviour and vocabulary'. If you are able to do this successfully you will be more able to lead or move that person in a new direction. Churches and Terry (2007: 54) argue that in order to be able to influence someone to do this 'you need to pace their current experience before you seek to lead them. The more you pace first, the more likely you are to be able to influence.' The skill they suggest here is being able to gradually move the balance towards leading the person. This strategy can be adopted when trying to move a student on from an entrenched position to a better position in behaviour management terms. We will look at rapport building in more detail in Chapter 5.

Prefacing

When you have a negative or correctional statement to make it is always best to try to preface this with a positive comment.

Peripheral praise

This is a particularly effective strategy to choose when you want a student to reflect on their behaviour. It is also one which does not allow any student challenge or dispute. If a learner is showing a lack of effort or poor behaviour, speak in turn to the students sitting on either side of them and give a praise statement to each. Then give a brief sideways glance to the target student, say nothing, and move away from them. This should have a powerful impact on their subsequent behaviour.

Paradoxical instructions

Sometimes learners will walk away from us when we are discussing an issue with them. This flight response can often be a natural reaction if they are being challenged on an issue, and sometimes it is used to show defiance. The easiest way to respond to this is to say 'That's OK, you go for a walk, but when we meet at the end of the day we will chat about this issue then'. This statement demonstrates that they are not defying you but are in fact carrying out your instructions.

Pre-suppositions

These are hidden meanings in the words we use. Often the first part of a sentence will presuppose a student will do what you have suggested. Churches and Terry (2007: 50) suggest that a particularly useful form in this instance is to use a double bind 'when you want to limit the possibilities that the person you are talking to will have'. An example of this would be 'Zak, would you like to begin by completing the questionnaire or writing up the results of the last task?' By stating several undeniable points we can set up a 'yes' set pattern where the student is more likely to agree to the statements we have made. We can then issue an instruction or direction. Ending a sentence with a 'yes' tag (e.g. a 'wouldn't it?' or 'isn't it?' statement together with a nod of the head) will make their compliance even more likely. Politicians and double-glazing salespeople will often use this strategy. Positive presuppositions can also be used to motivate students (e.g. 'This first section was the hardest part of the module'). This then presupposes that the rest of the work will be easier.

Reflection on practice

Make a list of five positive presuppositions you could use with learners to encourage and motivate them when they are finding their work challenging.

1 _____
   _____

2 _____
   _____

3 _____
   _____

---

4 _____

_____

5 _____

_____

Compare your list with that of another person in the group.

Ways to successfully manage students' controlling or distracting behaviours

- Students' behaviour can be used to mask their true feelings. Their challenging behaviour could be because they fear adults getting close to them. Avoid reacting immediately, use silence, and take a few deep breaths before responding. It may also give students time for reflection and to change their behaviour.

- Students can use 'chase me' behaviours which are designed to provoke an emotional response from you. They may attempt to do so by making a negative comment, smirking, or pushing furniture over. It is vital that we do not react immediately to this and instead choose the right time and place in which to address the issue.

- Students can attempt an entrapment strategy whereby they will try to get an excessively negative response from you or put words in your mouth. They may make negative comments to you. If that is the case thank them for expressing their views and say you will discuss these with them later on. This undermines their power play because they are not getting the response they expected.

- Students who are challenging will try to blame everyone else for their poor behaviour – the lecturer, their parents, or other students. Deflect the responsibility for their behaviour back to the student. Try to re-focus them by getting in their line of sight. Explain to them that they own their behaviour and they can change the consequences of it by choosing to modify their behaviour (refer to the section on secondary behaviour and smokescreening covered in Chapter 2).

When dealing with students who are displaying challenging behaviour try to keep in mind the following points.

- Avoid 'Venus Fly Trap' moments where you are drawn into a situation and into their behaviours. It is very easy to get involved in a power struggle here. Be objective and keep your responses low key.

- Keep to the point and do not let the classroom disruptors win. Act early to avoid a situation escalating. In your interactions be brief and positive.

- Try to keep these interactions private and audible only to the student involved. Doing so starves them of the 'oxygen of publicity' they were seeking from their peer group.

- Differentiate the serious from the trivial. Sometimes it is tactically better to ignore some behaviours in order to keep a lesson on track and then deal with these at a more appropriate time.

- When dealing with an incident try to avoid disturbing the rest of the class.

- Make your expectations clear to learners. Outline what you expect in the establishment phase of a session.

- Tune in to how a student is feeling before choosing from your repertoire of responses.

- If you reprimand a student who is held in high esteem in the group and their behaviour is checked, then the ripple effect from this will be strong and reflect well on your ability.

- When dealing with an incident leave a student's previous bad behaviour behind. Only respond to the here and now.

- An immediate intervention is more effective, such as moving a student to a different workplace in the room, parking them with a colleague in another room, or using 'Time Out' where they will spend time away in an area set up by college to reflect.

- Standing next to a student and asking if they would like some help might get them back on task and remove the need for a sanction.

- Standing behind them and saying nothing can also prove powerful – speaking would weaken the effect.

- Writing names on the board can be effective as well. For example, if a student's name has been written down three times by the end of a lesson then you would apply a sanction.

- If a sanction is warranted you must carry this out. Students have least respect for those staff who threaten punishments often but never give them. Remember that whatever you say you must do. Don't make disproportionate and unrealistic threats in the heat of the moment.

- The sanction could be as little as detaining the student for a few minutes at the end of a session, particularly when that lesson backs onto a break.

- The sanctions that students like least are those involving the loss of social time or their parents being contacted.

- Using incidental language, almost as an aside, can be a useful strategy. For example, if resources need to be cleared away you could say 'Some resources need to be cleared away. I would be most grateful if someone could help put them away so we can all make a prompt exit at the end of the lesson'.

Why not try this? Key scripts to use

When giving instructions to students or managing their behaviour we need to ensure we have a clear script we can use. Practise the following:

- Describe what you want them to do rather than not do. For example, say clearly 'Stop what you are doing, face this way, and listen'. Just think of your own reaction when you are told *not* to do something – most of us will still be tempted to do it.

- Focus on the required behaviour and sanction the behaviour not the student.

- Staying solution-focused is a good strategy to employ – 'We're in this together, let's try to find a solution'.

- Validating a student's feelings can be helpful – 'I can see you are upset'.

- When giving instructions to a student make sure these are followed by a 'thank you'. This will make it sound as if you expect compliance.

- Move around the room giving quiet instructions or comments in a low-key manner as this is a good way of gaining compliance.

- Try to avoid over-verbalising as saying too much can result in your message being weakened.

- Stay in control by initiating and ending your interactions with students. However, do try to avoid point-scoring with them. Sometimes it may be best to ignore certain comments. Be 'Teflon-coated' – nothing sticks.

- Having made a comment, give the student enough take-up time to comply. This is particularly important if they are angry.

- Use naming the rule, where you identify what it is you want – 'Sitting quietly … thanks'.

- Do not back students into a corner. Give them options. Allow them to save face.

- Give students direct choices based on the rules.

- A choices script to use with students can be very effective – 'Let's be very clear about this. As a member of staff at this college I am instructing you to [x]. You now have a choice. Either co-operate fully and follow my instructions or, if you choose not to, there will be a consequence of [x]'. If the student follows your instructions say 'Thank you for making the right choice'. If not, then say 'You have chosen to refuse my direct instruction. The consequence of your choice is …'. Your script should be delivered slowly and calmly to allow the student enough take-up time and also a sufficient amount of time to calm down.

- Maybes/partial agreements can help you to take the heat out of a situation. A script for a partial agreement could be as follows:

  Student: He gave me a dirty look.

  Lecturer: Maybe he did but I would really like you to [x].

  Student: Why have you got lines all over your face?

> *Lecturer:*   Maybe I have but [x].
>
> *Student:*   You are a bad lecturer.
>
> *Lecturer:*   Maybe I am but [x].

- When students say negative things to you, do not show that you are phased by their comments. Thank them for their criticism and suggest they continue with their work.

- When re-directing a student who is not conforming it may be necessary to use single and double whats (see below).

- A more direct approach may be to use direct rule statements: 'We've got a rule for asking questions and I expect you to use it. Thanks'.

- When issuing a consequence this needs to be one that:

    o is related to the inappropriate behaviour

    o has reasonableness (namely certainty and not severity). If you say a sanction will be applied, ensure that it is. It does not have to be a big sanction: simply detaining students for a few minutes at the end of a session is normally enough. Students will not respect members of staff who frequently threaten them with sanctions but do not issue them.

Single What

> *Lecturer:* What's the rule for when you want to ask a question?
>
> [Pause – await student response]
>
> *Lecturer:* Use it.
>
> [Pause]
>
> *Lecturer:* Thank you.

Double What

> *Lecturer:* What are you doing and what should you be doing now?
>
> [Pause – await student response]
>
> *Lecturer:* Go and do it.
>
> [Pause]
>
> *Lecturer:* Thank you.

When/Then:

> *Lecturer*: It's a shame when you shout out because then I can't hear other students' opinions. When you put your hand up I will listen to your opinion.

A more direct approach here may be to use direct rule statements: 'We've got a rule for asking questions and I expect you to use it. Thanks'.

Case Study A

As a lecturer you may well become involved in teaching in prisons or in Young Offender Institutions. A lecturer working in a Category C prison teaching literacy as a Skills for Life tutor has raised the following points which should be considered in relation to working in the Prison Education Service:

- Security

  - All classroom doors and cupboards will be locked behind you.

  - Prison Officers will be assigned to each block of classrooms to deal with any issues. Sometimes this can restrict certain activities: for example, movements associated with brain breaks may be thought of as threatening actions by students.

  - An alarm button can be found behind the tutor's desk.

  - You will not be able to leave the room once students arrive.

  - Any issues that happen must usually be reported to security via a slip system. There will be significant ramifications for prisoners if they misbehave. Being sent to prison officers will lead to disciplinary action and could also mean a loss of privileges (for example, the loss of television in a prisoner's cell).

  - You will have to think carefully about the lessons you plan and the sorts of materials you can incorporate (for example, you cannot issue pencil sharpeners as the blade may be concealed and used as a weapon).

  - Do not give out any personal details to students.

  - It can be daunting realising that the next big incident is never far away.

- Routines

  - There is rigidity to the system.

  - Each day's routine acts as a management system in itself.

(Continued)

(Continued)

- ○ Students will have a strict, prescribed and repetitive day.

- ○ Prisoners' controlled diet means there will be few bouts of food- and drink-induced hyperactivity after lunch as can be the case in college.

- ○ The length of lessons can be a problem – three hours with one 15-minute break is a challenge. Time slots will need to fit in with various operations in the prison. You could break a session up with quiz or filler activities. Some students will request toilet breaks more often than they should as a diversion.

- Students

  - ○ These will come from different parts of the country and will not have any affiliation with the rest of the group.

  - ○ You will be teaching a class of individuals rather than a group of friends, thus the dynamic that can cause challenges in a college setting will not be present.

  - ○ Students will arrive for a first session not fully realising what they are going to do: for example, if this involves literacy in Skills for Life they may well 'kick off' because they do not want to do this. It is important to sell them the benefits of learning literacy, including being able to read a story to their child or fill out benefit forms. In addition you could promise that once it is completed they can move on to their vocational choice e.g. Horticulture or Brickwork. Some learners will be concerned about appearing foolish because they have had negative learning experiences in school.

  - ○ Students will join and leave courses at different points as they will often be moved between prisons. This can cause problems with the management of learning.

  - ○ There will also be motivation issues with some students.

- Resources

  - ○ There will be no internet facilities available to support student learning.

In conclusion the tutor suggested that in reality relatively few issues usually arose and that there were many advantages to teaching in prison. For example, there were fewer behavioural problems compared to working in a college. He felt that some classes such as GCSE English were a pleasure to teach as students had specifically chosen to take these. Prison could also help some students to get their personal lives back on track, particularly if personal development qualifications were offered.

Points for reflection

1   Given the three-hour long lesson times in prison how would you adapt your lesson plans in order to motivate and keep the attention of your students in Prisoner Education?

2   What part do you think Prisoner Education plays in contributing to the wider rehabilitation scheme of a prison?

_____

_____

_____

3   Why do you think there are generally less behavioural problems in prison compared with college?

_____

_____

_____

Case Study B

Work-Based Learning

This Case Study has been based on an all-male group of work-based learning engineers. The following points were raised by a lecturer working with the group and the Work-Based Learning Provider.

Lecturer

- Some learners in the group were diligent and committed but they found it extremely difficult to produce written work.

- Most of the remainder of the group lacked commitment and were well behind in their college work. There was a distinct possibility that they would fail their assessment.

- Students found it difficult to manage situations and would throw tantrums and often storm off when faced with a challenge. They also found it hard to identify what triggered this behaviour.

- Many of the students displayed poor social behaviours and found positive interactions with other students, lecturers and employers extremely difficult.

- Some students arrived with alcohol on their breath and showed signs of having had very little sleep. This led to irritability and an inability to concentrate.

- They displayed immature behaviour towards female students and made inappropriate comments to them. Both sexes used mobile phones to dare each other to do stupid things.

- Some students were successful on placements and were quiet and not outgoing. However, in college their behaviour would be inappropriate and sometimes challenging. Their employer often found this hard to believe.

Employer

- Several students had a poor attention span and would simply walk away from work tasks and duties.

- Some students continually used their mobile phones. The company had contemplated installing a mobile phone signal jamming system in the work environment to stop this.

- Timekeeping was an issue for many students:

  - they arrived late at the start of the day

  - they took extended tea and lunch breaks

- Some of their work was slapdash and they did not give it enough attention to detail.

- Many had little regard for their employers and gave the impression that they did not care if they retained their jobs or not.

Points for reflection

1   What strategies would you use to develop a consistent approach to the way student behaviour is managed in both a college setting and a work-based learning setting?

_____
_____
_____

2   What systems need to be developed to ensure a closer working relationship between the college and employers?

_____
_____
_____

3   What would you do to improve students' motivation on work-based learning programmes?

_____
_____
_____

4   What would you do as a lecturer if you felt that an employer was not giving appropriate training on the placement and was attempting to use students as cheap labour?

5 What would you do if the employer complained that the college was not doing enough appropriate training on the day a student attended college for training?

_____

_____

_____

Key points

- The importance of the seven Ps:

  - Posture.

  - Pitch and tone.

  - Pacing.

  - Prefacing.

  - Peripheral praise.

  - Paradoxical instructions.

  - Pre-suppositions.

- Ways to manage students' controlling behaviours:

  - Avoid 'chase me' and entrapment.

  - Keep interactions low key and private.

  - Tune in to how they are feeling.

  - Tactically ignore some behaviours.

  - Use incidental language.

- Key scripts to use:

  - Broken record technique.

  - Choices.

(Continued)

(Continued)

- ○ Blocking secondary behaviour with the broken record technique.

- ○ Partial agreements/maybes.

- ○ Single and double whats.

- ○ What thens.

- Teaching in prisons will be different to working in a college environment. Points to consider:

  - ○ Sessions are of three hours duration and so it is essential to break up the session with a variety of activities.

  - ○ You need to sell the benefits of your subject.

  - ○ Students join and leave courses at different points.

  - ○ Resources are restricted, e.g. no internet facilities.

- Teaching on work-based programmes can lead to the need for close liaison with the employer to ensure that appropriate behaviour is displayed by the student in work-based and college-based settings.

CHAPTER 5

The importance of body language

In this chapter we will look at how we can use body language to successfully manage inappropriate behaviour. The body language we display will have a real impact on how successful we are in managing behaviour. If we are talking tough, does our body language confirm or contradict this? Is there a congruence between our verbal and non-verbal communication? We can also read students' body language to give us clues about what they are really thinking and feeling. Ribbens and Thompson (2002) confirm this when they state: 'non-verbal communication provides clues to how people think and feel'.

Body language contributes a great deal to how we communicate. According to Mehrabian (1981), in the context of communicating feelings and attitude, 7 per cent of any message will be conveyed in the words spoken, 38 per cent in paralanguage/vocal tone, and 55 per cent through a non-verbal form, particularly facial expressions. Body language betrays our emotions or thoughts and is delivered and read unconsciously. However, words can take on greater significance: for example, when a command statement is made in a workshop where a student is about to do something which will endanger them or others, or when an emergency message is given out in a shopping mall to evacuate the area. There is a need therefore to analyse how we appear when we are involved in disciplinary interactions with students. Sometimes by rehearsing our response in front of a mirror or video camera we can easily analyse our body language and review how we conveyed a message.

The importance of the four Cs

Based on work by Pease (2000: 14–16) and my own experience in the classroom, when we are looking at body language we need to remember the four Cs (Vizard, 2004b):

- Clusters.

- Congruence.

- Context.

- Culture.

Clusters

Reading too much into a single piece of body language is a mistake as a little knowledge can be a dangerous thing. In addition, there can be several interpretations for the same type of body language. When looking at a student check for clusters of body language that have the same meaning and interpretation. For example, if their Adam's Apple is jumping, their ankles are locked, and their shoulders are hunched, this could be a sign of apprehension and anxiety. When we are working with students we need to make sure that we cluster our body language to ensure a consistent message is being given.

Congruence

Look for congruence between student's verbal and non-verbal communication. For example, uncertainty in the voice, together with rubbing of their eyes and nose, may convey that they are lying. We need to ensure that we show congruence between our verbal and non-verbal communication. Some staff will often display a lack of congruence (for example, by speaking firmly and displaying weak body language or vice versa). Students will quickly tune in to this and see it as a sign of weakness. In addition, if we are too rehearsed and display overcongruence, whereby we will appear too rehearsed, this can also cause problems. James (2008: 17) confirms this and says overcongruence will show if 'your tone is too strong and your movements are too exaggerated ... overcongruent communications are the enemy of sincerity, so avoid them at all costs'.

Context

Some non-verbal communication will occur in a direct relationship to the context in which an individual finds themself. Someone sitting with their arms and legs crossed and looking down could be interpreted as displaying negative body language, but in reality this could be someone in a room where the air-conditioning has been set at too low a temperature and the 'negative' body language is to avoid the onset of frost-bite!

Culture

As a certain television advert for a bank told us a few years ago, remember that the same gesture will mean various things to people in different parts of the world.

For example, in some cultures:

- Smiling is a startle response to being told off.

- Staring at someone is the most disrespectful thing you could do.

- Standing close to someone is a natural response when feeling guilty.

Some of the key areas relating to non-verbal communication are discussed below.

Eye contact

Appropriate use of eye contact is the key to successful behaviour management. As Borg (2008: 38) states 'More communication is conveyed through the eyes than any other part of the body'.

- Using eye contact can engage someone's attention, display our interest, and indicate our intent.

- When initially meeting and greeting students at the classroom doorway at the beginning of each lesson we need to have firm eye contact with them.

- At the start of the lesson we need to scan the whole group. Our eyes should scan across the room, our head should move slowly from left to right or vice versa. We must keep our head in its first position and scan, moving our eyes fully from left to right or vice versa before moving our head to the next position to complete the scan. This action shows real confidence. Using eye contact can engage student attention and will indicate our awareness of all students. We should also engage in longer eye contact with those students who are the influencers in a group. However, we must also avoid staring too much as this can create a perception of hostility or threat.

- Lecturers who manage behaviour well will use eye contact in a confident manner. They will adopt smooth and slow eye movements and not be phased by looking at a student for an extended period (being careful not to turn it into a staring competition). Kuhnke (2007: 81) states that if you wish 'to be taken seriously keep your gaze in the triangular area between the eyes and the centre of the forehead. As long as your eyes remain in that space and you keep control of the interaction ... you're someone who means business'.

- Remember that when people are in conversation they will look at each other between 40 and 75 per cent of the time, according to Ribbens and Thompson (2002: 13). Any longer than that can be seen as unsettling, embarrassing, or threatening. However, a longer stare may be necessary with some students. When talking we will maintain eye contact for 40 per cent of the time and we will have to look away to think of the next point. When listening we will engage in eye contact for over 75 per cent of the time, according to Ribbens and Thompson (2002: 13). We will also spend about 31 per cent of our time engaging in mutual gazing. The average gaze lasts 2.95 seconds and the average mutual gaze about 1.8 seconds in most contexts.

- Do not give off any frightened or passive messages (for example, staring into the distance or looking at the ground). This eye dip movement is a submissive gesture and shows reluctance to enter into an interaction.

- Avoid the eye shuttle where you flick your eyes from side to side without any head movement. This is a startle response and also a submissive gesture, where someone is taking in everything happening around them, and it can appear as though they are looking for an escape route.

- When moving around the room a sideways glance towards a student can be controlling as it will generate an attitude of doubt or suspicion. Moving into a student's space with a look is also effective in managing behaviour about 90 per cent of the time.

- If a student is misbehaving move into the student's line of sight and establish eye contact with a stare (by doing this you will establish a clear message that you expect that student to change their behaviour). Give your direction and then move away to allow them sufficient take-up time to conform. In these circumstances try to avoid extended and unnecessary eye contact.

- To show your approval it is important when talking to a student not to gaze off, concentrate on paperwork, or look at your watch. These non-verbal cues will show dislike or disagreement.

Positioning

At the beginning of a lesson

- When speaking to the class stand in a position where you can scan or 'lighthouse' the whole group.

- Remember that it is important psychologically for you to be able to see the entire class.

- Think about your power position. This relates to whether you are left- or right-handed. Right-handed lecturers are normally right-eye dominant and would be in their 'power position' if they stood in a position in the room where they could scan the room from left to right (see Figure 5.1).

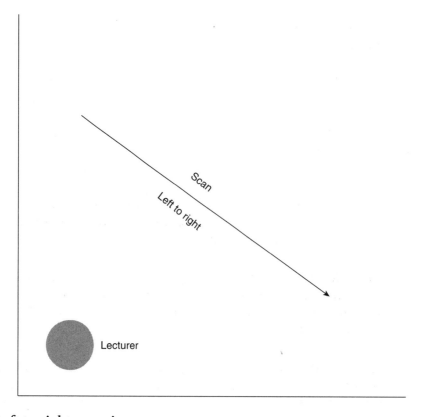

Figure 5.1   Left to right scanning

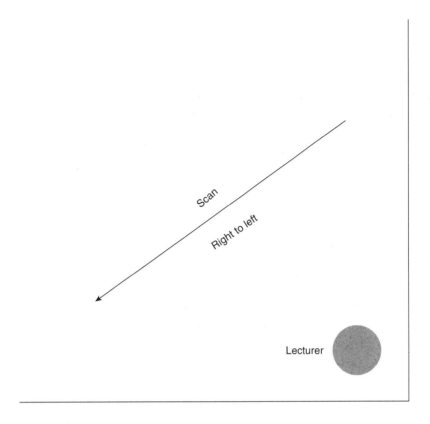

Figure 5.2   Right to left scanning

- Left-handed lecturers are normally left-eye dominant and would be in their 'power position' if they stood in a position in the room where they could scan the room from right to left (see Figure 5.2).

- Some students will be aware that lecturers can sometimes have a blindspot just to their right if they are left-eye dominant or to their left if right-eye dominant. Some challenging students will be aware of this and will then gravitate towards those areas.

- It is vital to remember the 'psychological geography' mentioned in Chapter 4.

Patrolling

- It is essential that you patrol your territory frequently – you should avoid having no-go areas in your learning environment. Remember to visit all areas of the room.

- When settling a group as they begin to work it may be best to patrol your classroom by moving around the perimeter of the room. This will keep the maximum number of students within your gaze while they are settling into their task.

- A good position to stand in for periods of time is at the back of the room. Students, without the aid of wing mirrors on their desks, will then be put at a psychological disadvantage.

Proximity

- When teaching it may be necessary to walk around the room and move into those areas where problem behaviours are developing. Going towards a student and putting your hand on their desk, but without stopping talking to the group, can have a powerful effect.

- If notes are being passed around, stand next to the student holding the note and say nothing. The likely outcome of this is that the note will be put away.

- Standing behind a student who is not working, slightly within their personal space bubble but without saying anything, can be highly effective.

- Regarding physical closeness, Pease (2000: 20–21), based on work by Hall (1959), suggested that each individual has a personal space bubble of 46 centimetres – the 'intimate zone'. If anyone goes inside of this space we can feel threatened. When a person becomes angry the boundary of this space is likely to increase, so it is important when dealing with students that we do not appear to be invading their personal space bubble which might then provoke a confrontation.

Level

- Standing over a student whilst they are seated can put you at a psychological advantage but it is probably better to avoid this as it can be very intimidating. Sitting at the same level, or even better crouching at a slightly lower level, can lead to more effective communication and reduce the likelihood of increasing conflict.

Posture

- Posture is very important, as we discussed in Chapter 4, so try to stand upright with a straight back when working with a class of students during the formal parts of the lesson and when dealing with disciplinary matters. Avoid at all costs standing and stooping slightly with your head down and leg bent as this will create the impression you are lacking in confidence.

- Standing with your feet slightly apart is a confident posture. A closed gait can show a lack of confidence.

- Stand with an open posture. Avoid closed body language, such as folded arms.

Barrier positions

Barrier gestures can be unhelpful when dealing with challenging students. Some examples of barrier gestures include:

- folded or crossed arms, which suggest defensiveness or hostility

- having one arm across the body, which shows nervousness or a lack of self-confidence

- holding books or a bag in front of you as a barrier, which suggests nervousness and defensiveness.

Bodily orientation

The angle and direction in which your body points is said to indicate your feelings. If you point yourself away from the person it could be perceived that you have a negative attitude towards them. In conflict situations it is vital to avoid standing face to face as this can inflame the conflict. It is best to stand at right angles to the person in these situations. However, in some situations it is better to stand leaning slightly forward and square on to make more of your stature.

Head lowering or tilting

Submissive people will frequently lower their head or tilt it to one side. This is a sign of appeasement and we should try to avoid doing this in front of students.

Facial expressions

The phrase 'they gave me a dirty look' is often given as the trigger for conflict. Roffey (2004) gives further emphasis to the importance of looks and facial expressions, indicating that 'our faces are mirrors to our minds'. Collett (2004: 54–57) suggests we all have certain 'ticks and tells' that can give away what we are thinking. These include the following.

- Frowning and raising our eyebrows can indicate disapproval. Shaking or nodding our heads is a way to indicate our disapproval or approval, respectively.

- Increased blinking is a sign of anxiety. When our mind is aroused or racing there will be an increase in our normal blink rate: 'Our normal blinking rate is about 20 blinks per minute, but it can increase to four or five times that figure when we feel under pressure' (Collett, 2004: 290).

- Narrowing our eyes is also a sign of control or dominance. Doing so gives the impression we are looking through the slit in a helmet. Clint Eastwood, in the 'Dollar' series of movies, used this expression frequently.

- Lowering our eyebrows gives the impression of dominance because it creates a more confrontational stare (when angry we will tend to lower our eyebrows).

- Raising our eyebrows, as well as signalling our disapproval, can also indicate submissiveness.

- If our mouth is set in a resolute position without a smile this can be very controlling – the horizontal mouth shape. Symmetrical smiles are seen as sincere. Asymmetrical smiles are seen as insincere.

- Raising our head and pushing our bottom teeth beyond the top set is seen as a common gesture of defiance or control that is used in confrontation. This 'jaw thrust' is also a sign of dominance.

Non-verbal cueing

You can practise a range of non-verbal cues to give to students. These carry a clear unspoken message, direction, or reminder. They will also save on lesson disruptions and wear and tear of your voice. Lecturers in practical areas are particularly effective in using non-verbal cues in their voice-sapping teaching environments.

We all use a range of non-verbal cues with students and some of the best examples are those used by learning support workers when they signal to learners across a room non-verbally. With the slightest movement of their hand, a tilt of the head or a facial expression they can signal their wishes or responses to a student. In workshops and practical areas, having a repertoire of non-verbal cues is essential.

Some cues of this type would include:

- Smiling and nodding in response to a student – this shows our interest and approval.

- Finger to lips – this acts as a request for quiet.

- Finger pointing downwards – this means sit down.

- Hands moving away from the top of the head – this means remove hat.

- Pointing to watch – this says take-up time is over and time is now being wasted.

- Clicking fingers/clapping hands – this is to get the attention of the group.

- Holding arm in the air – this means students must do the same in turn to show they are ready.

- Rotating hands – this says hurry up.

In our consideration of non-verbal cueing, both here and in the rest of this chapter, we need to be aware that some students with certain conditions and syndromes – for example those on the autistic spectrum – will not find it easy to decode non-verbal communications in others. They may not be able to interpret gestures, so utilising these strategies with such students may meet with limited success.

Reflection on practice

Think about the range of non-verbal cues you use with students. List these and give each a score on their effectiveness: score 1 for not very effective and score 5 for those that are very effective.

Compare your scores with another person and work out a Top Five for your most effective non-verbal cues.

Our Top Five

1 _____
  _____

2 _____
  _____

3 _____
  _____

4 _____
  _____

5 _____
  _____

Gestures

We will often use certain gestures to support what we are saying. These can help us to be more successful in our ability to manage inappropriate behaviours. However, some gestures can be at an unconscious level which may give away our emotions or true feelings and thus prove to be a hindrance. Below are some examples of both of these categories – firstly gestures that are unhelpful:

- Affect displays and adaptors – for example, body tics such as frequent switches and movements in the body, touching the face, fiddling with objects such as glasses.

- Minute gestures – for example, lip pursing, slight eyebrow movement, and nostril flaring all give away our true feelings.

- Displacement gestures – for example, when we are feeling uncomfortable we will stroke our hair, tap our fingers, and keep adjusting our clothes.

Gestures which can be helpful:

- Illustrators – as educators we are usually good at using these. They are gestures which reinforce what we are saying – we will often gesture with our palms to make a point.

We will also use power lifts where we use a pointed finger to guide learners' attention to where we want them to look (for example, to information on a screen).

- Signature gestures – these are used by competent practitioners who have a confident pose: these can be idiosyncratic, but they can also set you apart from other staff. Sir Winston Churchill's victory sign was a famous example of a signature gesture.

Reflection on practice

In pairs, stand three metres apart facing each other and select a topic for each person to talk about for two minutes. Each person then takes it in turn to present their topic. For the duration of the activity the speaker should use illustrators and signature gestures.

At the end of the activity you should discuss the illustrators and signature gestures used.

If you notice any unhelpful gestures being used, identify these and discuss them.

Relaxed position

Try to appear relaxed when you are faced with difficult students. They will be trying to get a reaction from you by attempting to identify your 'hot buttons'. For this they will be reading your body language closely. Ensure you appear relaxed by:

- asymmetrically positioning your limbs

- maintaining openness in your arm position

- using open palm gestures

- using a sideways lean and tilt for your head position

- adopting a more reclining position when seated.

Rapport building

When dealing with angry and inappropriately behaving students it is necessary that you think about how to develop a rapport with them.

- Angry students will speak using words showing their sensory preference. Listen to this and mirror the language of their sensory preference back to them. For example, if a student tells you 'I can't see the point' they have a visual sensory preference and therefore you should reply using visual language: 'Let's look at it again'. Alternatively a student with an auditory sensory preference might say 'I am frustrated because you are not listening to me'. Thus a suitable response on your part could be 'I hear what you have said': you could then paraphrase some of the things the student had just said. And once again, someone with a kinaesthetic sensory preference might say 'It feels like nobody likes me in this group', whereby your response might be, 'Hang on a minute' – followed by examples of where you and other students have been supportive of them.

- Use mirroring, matching, and cross-over matching of students' body language:

  ○ Matching involves adopting the same body language as the student. If they rest their left hand on their right shoulder you should do the same.

  ○ Mirroring involves providing a mirror image, so you would need to put your right hand onto your left shoulder.

  ○ Cross-over matching involves you matching their breathing rate (breathing in unison) or responding to their blink breathing rate by tapping your hands on your side or tapping feet at the same rate. If you do this then the student should unconsciously feel a sense of connection with you.

- Use mismatching and breaking the rapport. This is the opposite of matching and can be utilised in certain situations where you wish to indicate to the student that you have had enough of the stance they are taking on an issue. To do this you need to break eye contact, look at your watch, gaze over their shoulder, and use facial tells – raising your eyebrows, changing the sound of your voice, or walking away.

- Listen to their speech patterns and try to adopt their rate of speech, using similar intonations and rhythms.

- Use similar sentence length and colloquialisms.

- Practise Interactional Synchronizing, whereby you move in a similar way.

- Build rapport through gaze by directly looking at the student for two or three seconds.

- Try to gauge a student's emotional state and establish an emotional rapport by acknowledging their feelings and matching their strength of feeling in your voice.

Once you have tuned in to the student's emotional state and matched it, you will be in a better position to attempt to change their mood. By changing your behaviour you can lead them slightly in the direction that you would like them to move. If you want to gain an indication of any changes that are taking place look into their eyes: their pupil size might then indicate (in the correct lighting conditions) if they are in a more positive frame of mind. Large dilated pupils will indicate this. Note that if their pupils are still small then they are still feeling angry.

Reflection on practice

In pairs, decide on a topic you wish to discuss for five minutes. For the first half of the discussion attempt to mismatch the body language of your partner and break your rapport with them. Then for the second half use all the strategies outlined above to re-establish that rapport. At the end of the activity discuss how you felt during the two halves. How could you use rapport building strategies with learners in the classroom?

_____

_____

_____

Use of silence

Silence is a very powerful tool in your behaviour management toolbox. Think of the dramatic effect in a theatre when an actor uses silence – exactly the same will occur if this is included in disciplinary interactions.

- If you ask for silence, wait until you get it. Talking over student chatter will severely undermine your authority. Use a stopwatch to time delay and hold back students at the end of the session.

- When we start a lesson or are about to be involved in a disciplinary interaction with students it is important that we wait for silence. This same wait for silence should also be observed when we bring students together during the lesson and before we dismiss them at the end.

- When giving a command or becoming involved in a disciplinary interaction, tactical pausing is a good strategy to use. Use a student's first name, then pause for up to five seconds, then make your statement. In the tactical pause it is essential that you maintain eye contact.

- Moving into the student's territory and standing behind them saying nothing can be utilised to indicate to the student that he or she has been noticed.

- If there is poor behaviour look at the student without saying anything as this can be unnerving for them.

- Sometimes it will be necessary to tactically ignore some minor incidents of poor behaviour because responding to every incident, no matter how minor, can prove extremely disruptive.

- If a student makes an inappropriate/disruptive comment, silence can be just as effective as a verbal reprimand for indicating to them that they have not been behaving appropriately.

Key points to remember

- Importance of the four Cs – Clusters, Congruence, Context and Culture.

- Eye contact – sustain firm eye contact with students.

- Positioning – when teaching stand in a position where you can scan the whole group. Stand in your 'power position' – this is related to eye dominance.

- Patrol your area:

  ○ Do not have no-go areas.

  ○ On occasions standing at the back of the room can be highly effective.

- Proximity:

  ○ Move around the room and stand close to those students displaying inappropriate behaviour.

  ○ Try not to invade the 46 cm personal space bubble.

- Level – your interactions may be more successful if you crouch or kneel next to a student. Standing over a seated student will appear as controlling.

- Bodily orientation – the angle and direction your body points will indicate your feelings.

- Facial expressions – lowering eyebrows, narrowing eyes, jaw thrusts and horizontal mouth shape are examples of controlling expressions.

- Non-verbal cues – have a repertoire of clearly understood non-verbal cues.

- Importance of gestures – this includes affect displays, adaptors, minute and displacement gestures, illustrator and signature gestures.

- Practise ways by which you can build a rapport with students.

- Use of silence – when dealing with challenging students tactical pausing (naming the student and pausing for five seconds before giving a direction) can be a powerful tool.

CHAPTER 6

Managing anger and confrontation

Understanding why students become angry and confrontational

Everyone has some anger inside them; it is an explosive energy which is required for self-preservation. However, some students can find themselves unable to cope with the demands of their situation and respond with anger. Sometimes transferring to a college can be traumatic – going to a large institution with older learners and a different curriculum can disrupt learners – even with the best induction programmes. In addition, when students display anger towards lecturers they are using displacement. Often by our actions and social tone we may remind them of someone outside college who may have been extremely negative or abusive towards them. Therefore inappropriate feelings will often be displaced onto us by that student.

Many learners will not have the emotional intelligence necessary to decode the non-verbal and verbal communication that is occurring around them in order to understand when situations are likely to result in conflict. Added to this they may not have enough of a vocabulary to negotiate and discuss these situations. Students are good observers, but they are not always able to interpret the world around them. Many potential conflicts could be avoided by effective communication.

Students who misbehave will be doing so in order to gain the attention of their peers and adults. These learners will have very low self-esteem and feelings of inadequacy. A number will also have inappropriate problem-solving styles and will be attempting to learn appropriate ways to behave.

Remember that 'all behaviour is learnt'.

Analysing the physiology of anger

Located at the top of the spinal cord and at the base of the brain, our reptilian brain is triggered when there is a threat of danger. According to Fisher (2005), this reptilian part of the brain is concerned with individual survival and it developed whilst we were still amphibians. It comes into action when we sense danger, increasing our heart rate and sending adrenalin surging through our body, and it propels us into a high state of alert where we are ready to respond with a fight, flight, freeze, or flock response. Fisher (2005: 48) also suggests this part of the brain can be 'stimulated by triggers related to deep-seated unresolved traumatic events in our life', as cortisol released at the time of the earlier event suppresses the hippocampus which gives a context to the event. These strong emotional memories remain stored and can easily become a trigger for overreactions in our own present lives. They can also impair our brain whereby we lose the ability to think and reason effectively. Blood chemicals tell us to act and the message is so strong that our neo-cortex (the top part of our brain where we do most of our logical thinking and planning) cannot operate properly. As a result as individuals we are flooded with feelings and cannot think properly. Because of this we can become vulnerable and are more likely to be unpredictable, often displaying outbursts of extreme behaviour.

The neural links between emotional and cognitive sites are greater in number than those from the cognitive to the emotional centres. It therefore takes longer for the thinking site to send back the information that the situation is not serious. Hence many people will respond in an inappropriate manner because of the time-lag involved. They are literally taken over by the emotion they are experiencing.

Vizard (2009: 99) expands on this point by stating that 'neural pathways develop which link the reptilian brain directly with the impulsive areas of the brain such as the amygdala. When faced with a problem, messages are sent to the reptilian part of the brain rather than to the thinking area – the neo-cortex – and can lead to inappropriate responses and a lack of self-control'. In fact Australian scientists at the University of Melbourne have found that the amygdala is bigger in students who are prone to prolonged and aggressive arguments. Think about our reaction to confrontational behaviour. When aroused, we tend to give an animal-like response: we become locked into a pattern of behaviour that sees increased states of arousal on both sides of the argument and irrationality takes over as our hormones kick in. How often have you observed someone in a conflict situation, when all their rational thoughts seem to have disappeared? They will be red faced, eyes bulging, invading someone else's personal space.

Other types of unhelpful responses that might be triggered would include:

- shouting

- not listening to others' views

- bringing up past unrelated misdemeanours

- standing toe to toe/face to face

- raising the voice in response to another's shouting

- allowing conflict to occur in a public forum

- using aggressive non-verbal communication (for example, pointing fingers in someone's face)

- flailing arms

- using aggressive facial expressions (for example, showing teeth).

Key phases of anger

These five phases have been described by Long and Fogell (1999) as comprising an 'anger mountain'.

1 Trigger phase

Initially there will be a trigger which will signal a perceived danger or problem. The hormone adrenalin will then be secreted.

2 Build-up phase

As we become more aroused we will tend to lose our ability to think rationally. Our emotional arousal is energising and this makes us sharp and ready for action.

3 Crisis phase

This is when we reach the summit of our anger mountain. Adrenalin will be coursing through our veins and we will reflect the hostile messages we may be getting. For example:

- by standing square on

- by inflating our lungs so our chest is bigger

- by making hostile eye contact

- by using our arms as weapons.

This is an extreme reaction but excessively aggressive behaviour can be seen as normal behaviour in abnormal circumstances.

4 Recovery phase

As the adrenalin surge drains away we will move into the recovery phase. However, sometimes we may have additional possible outbursts when more adrenalin is secreted. This will lead to excessively aggressive behaviour once again. When viewing CCTV footage of street crime, this is the phase when an aggressor will return to the victim they have just attacked and carry out a further frenzied attack – in this additional outburst the aggressor's anger knows no boundaries.

5 Post-event depression

After this surge of adrenalin most of us will feel very low and we can suffer temporarily from post-event depression.

In the first three phases of anger we may display the following signs:

- Our facial colour deepens.

- We will breathe faster.

- We will perspire more.

- We will have dilated pupils.

- We will speak more loudly and rapidly.

- We will become agitated and fidgety and move faster.

- We will tense our muscles, have a contorted face, and clench our fists.

- We will have tightly closed lips.

- We will have hunched shoulders and a stiff rigid posture.

- We will be easily distracted and unfocused.

- We will use aggressive posturing and point our fingers.

General strategies to use to reduce angry and confrontational behaviour

- Attempt to anticipate inappropriate behaviour by looking for signs and triggers in the student and in yourself.

- Try to remain calm when faced with someone who is angry as it is important to listen to what they say and acknowledge their feelings.

- Set the rhythm for the discussion with your first response. Respond rather than react. When responding make sure you do so constructively.

- Always explain to students the reasons for your actions.

- Show respect towards students and do not belittle or humiliate them.

- Permit students some dignity. If necessary give time and space for both of you to calm down.

- Sometimes it will be better to give a clear instruction and then move away from a student. Make it clear that you have the expectation that compliance will occur.

- Do not get pulled into a power struggle – keep your responses low key and do not allow the situation to escalate.

- Do not take things personally. Do not become defensive.

- Try to keep the situation in perspective.

- Try to persuade the other person to think positively about the situation. Help them to reframe negative thoughts and give these a positive spin.

- Show genuine concern and help the student to take control of the situation.

- Use pauses between responses. Using a form of tactical pausing can reduce the chances of confrontation and also shows respect as this demonstrates that you are reflecting on what they are saying.

- Remember that silence can be very effective.

- Convey non-aggressive intentions in your body language – avoid waving your arms as this can exacerbate the confrontation.

- When reading non-verbal communication in students we can easily become misled. Do not read single examples of non-verbal communication – always read 'gesture clusters'. Look for congruence between non-verbal and verbal forms of communication.

- Avoid having an emotional reaction to misbehaviour. Put up a wall between yourself and what the student is doing.

- Avoid excessive eye contact as this can be seen as threatening and challenging. Allow the student to look away. Standing at right angles to or alongside the student will help to avoid issues relating to eye contact.

- Avoid squaring up, invading their personal space (46cm), and making any threatening movements. Remember that appearing to retreat by moving away from the student can lead to problems.

- Do not copy their mood. For example, if they shout and you then shout louder, this can lead to an upward spiral of confrontational behaviour. Reflect an increase in emotional level to show that you are really concerned.

- Try to be solution-focused and allow the student to save face. Give them an escape route.

- Show that you are willing to accept a compromise, a solution that is acceptable to all and allows everyone to feel a winner. Making token concessions can be worthwhile, for example by admitting that they may have a point (known as the 1 per cent technical error strategy).

- Use inclusive language: 'we all get angry so it's OK to feel this way – we will certainly be able to find a solution'. This can prove useful as some learners will become scared by their extreme behaviour.

- Avoid trying to resolve the situation whilst the student is still angry. Giving them time out to reflect can be a useful strategy, particularly if they are not in the right mental state or the conditions are not suitable. Buying a period of time for reflection is important so try to utilise a time-out strategy.

- Avoid the 'oxygen of publicity' generated by public exchanges by taking the discussion somewhere private (but not away from a third party, otherwise you may be vulnerable). The situation is likely to become worse if it is acted out in front of a student's peers.

- Respect students' right to disagree and have different opinions to yours.

- Using attention diverters with distractions, real or imagined, can be a way of breaking the cycle of anger. For example, stand and look out of the window and say nothing – you may find that soon the student will join you in looking out of the same window.

- Sometimes you may need to use wrong-footing tactics and behave in a way that is different from what the student would normally expect from you.

- Think about what you will do in certain situations beforehand and produce scripts for these. Use friendly gestures. Do not point. Use the palms of your hands or place your hands by your side.

- Try to establish a rapport by matching and mirroring students' body language and listening to the language of their sensory preference (refer to Chapter 5).

- Stay in control of yourself by checking your body language and speech volume. Keep clear of power struggles and avoid hostile remarks where sarcasm and ridicule are used.

- When in a conflict situation it is sometimes easy to make idle threats that can never be followed through. Use certainty not severity – say what you mean and mean what you say.

- Use humour to relieve the tension of the situation.

- Avoid the 'Bad day/I am in a mood' syndrome that all staff can suffer from given the pressures they face.

Reflection on practice

Make a list of five strategies you would normally use with an angry and confrontational student.

1 _____
_____

2 _____
_____

3 _____
_____

(Continued)

(Continued)

4 _____
_____

5 _____
_____

Compare your list with a partner.

Case Study

Within one group of learners on a Return to Learn course there is a female student in her forties who has a negative attitude to the lecturer. She:

- is extremely challenging, argumentative and confrontational

- frequently questions her authority in an attempt to undermine it

- has a smug attitude and tries to catch the lecturer out by asking obscure questions

- expects the lecturer to give up a large quantity of time at the end of the session to help her

- has alienated the rest of the group by her extreme behaviour.

With a partner discuss which strategies you would use to manage this student's behaviour.

_____
_____
_____

How students express their anger

How students express their anger in a conflict situation can have a lot to do with their anger styles. Although anger styles are learned they are deeply ingrained and automatic, almost like reflexes.

Signs of a student becoming angry

In dealing with conflict it is helpful to be aware of some of the danger signs that indicate when conflict may be about to arise. A student may demonstrate the following behaviours:

- Unwilling to communicate.

- Looking away when you speak.

- Pacing around and unwilling to remain in their seat.

- Outbursts of temper.

- Frequently repeating certain phrases.

- Laughing in a false, sarcastic way.

- Appearing to perspire heavily.

- Shortness of breath or rapid breathing.

- Unable to settle down to work.

- Appears agitated.

- Easily distracted.

- Bulging eyes/narrow pupils.

- A stiff, rigid posture.

- Rapid body movements.

'Acting in' and 'acting out'

Based upon work by Schmidt (1993), Long and Fogell (1999) suggested that students would express their anger and challenge by 'acting in' or 'acting out'. The categories they presented are discussed below.

Acting in

Students who 'act in' attack themselves with self-damaging behaviour. They appear anxious, depressed, withdrawn, passive and unmotivated. There is an apparent irrational refusal to respond and co-operate. Two types of 'acting in' roles are:

- Stuffers:

  - hold in their anger and deny they are angry

  - avoid confrontation at all costs

  - suffer from depression and illnesses.

- Withdrawers:

  - express their anger by withdrawing from others

  - protect themselves from the cause of the anger by withdrawing, whilst also punishing those who caused it.

When you are working with Stuffers and Withdrawers remember to:

- mirror how they act and model appropriate strategies they could use to help themselves

- enable them to use positive affirmations – positive statements to raise their self-esteem at problem times

- help them to log incidents where they withdrew or held their anger and give them alternative approaches for the next occasion

- use dramatherapy to help them – use of story is also a powerful tool in emotional literacy.

Acting out

Students who 'act out' tend to be aggressive, threatening, demanding of attention and disruptive, and will also prevent others from working. Two types of acting out roles are:

- Blamers:

  o have little belief that they can make things better for themselves

  o blame others for their angry feelings

  o may tease and name call.

- Exploders:

  o express their anger through direct and immediate confrontation

  o will have a short fuse and be physically or verbally aggressive towards peers and adults.

When you are working with Blamers and Exploders remember to:

- provide regular contact with a mentor or behavioural assistant

- use a positive restitution approach, where the aggressor has to meet their victim and make it up with them

- focus the reprimand on the behaviour not the student

- use behaviour modification strategies to recognise and praise them when they get it right.

Fisher (2005), quoting work by Lee (1993), identified four anger styles that individuals display. Fisher also added on a fifth style of his own, 'the Winder-Upper'. These are as follows:

- *The Intimidator:* Seeks to control others by using fear – through adopting an aggressive standpoint.

- *The Interrogator:* Seeks to control others by using manipulation – through finding fault and making people feel self-conscious and guilty.

- *Poor Me:* Seeks to control others by using guilt – through implying they are not doing enough for them.

- *Distancer:* Seeks to control others by using distance – through remaining detached, unapproachable and vague.

- *The Winder-Upper:* Seeks to control others by using humour – through joking, teasing or mocking others.

Students tend to opt for one particular way of managing their behaviour. When we are supporting learners in managing their anger and confrontation effectively we need to get them to understand the physical signs both in themselves and others that will show when they are about to lose their temper. To do this we must:

- give them specific intervention strategies that they can implement in order to reduce their feelings of anger

- help them develop relaxation/stress reduction techniques that will assist with this.

Support and strategies we can give students

Some examples of the support we can give include:

- *Dramatherapy:* Through music and drama we can help students in understanding how to identify signs of anger and control their feelings. We can also give them an active vocabulary that they can utilise to negotiate in such situations.

- *Mirroring and modelling:* Gaining students' permission to mirror their non-verbal and verbal communication when they are getting angry might be a useful strategy. If you can mirror some of the signs this will increase their awareness of when exactly they are becoming angry. After doing so model some strategies that they might use to reduce their feeling of anger: such as breathing exercises, counting to ten, progressive muscle tensing and relaxation.

- *'Fire drills':* Give students various strategies that they can follow in conflict situations. Encourage them to rehearse what to do, particularly how they should react to an angry student in the classroom.

- *Developing positive self-talk:* Ask students to list four or five statements that they think might assist them when faced with another person's anger. This will help them to diffuse the chances of a conflict developing, for example:

- ○ 'I am not responsible for this person's feelings'.

- ○ 'People say things they don't mean when they are angry'.

- ○ 'Who makes me angry? I am the only person who can make me angry'.

- ○ 'I can reduce the tension by remaining calm'.

- *Relaxation techniques*: Ask students to practise the following:

  - ○ Progressive muscle relaxation – students need to tense and relax all muscle groups in their body in turn, from toes to neck and then from neck to toes.

  - ○ Visualisation – have students focus on an image of a very special place with happy memories. Suggest they use a detective-style magnifying glass to enlarge the scene and make the colours brighter. This will intensify the feeling. As they do this they should hold their thumb and forefinger together. Their mind will then be anchored in a location where they felt good and this will have a calming influence. Whenever they feel anxious or that there is anger rising they can anchor themselves by holding their forefinger and thumb together. Their mind will then associate that particular gesture with a positive feeling. Staff can also use this technique to anchor themselves when they are anxious or feeling stressed.

  - ○ Breathing for relaxation – help students to develop a deep breathing cycle.

  - ○ Tension releasers – provide objects for students to use that will allow them to release their stress (for example, stress balls).

- *Changing negative feelings:* Help students to reframe their negative feelings. Many angry students will have very low levels of self-esteem and fragile egos. If someone pushes or knocks into them in the corridor they will believe that that person wanted to hurt them or start a fight. We need to develop more neutral thoughts in students: perhaps the person lost their balance or they were not looking where they were going. Note that this is a long-term process that will ultimately help students.

- *Reflecting on the causes of conflict:* Try to help students to reflect on the causes of their anger. What is it that triggers them into anger and conflict? Ask them to keep an Anger Diary and record any incidents of anger and the triggers for these. Work through this with them and develop individual strategies they could adopt in response to these triggers.

- *Developing 'I' statements:* This helps learners to rationalise their behaviour and gives them a script to use with the other person in the conflict (for example, 'When you do [x] (behaviour), I feel upset (feeling) because I cannot do my work (effect). I would like to [x] (proposed solution)').

- *Reframing:* Students who behave badly tend to have extremely low self-esteem and a very negative self-image; they think that 'everyone in the world has it in for me'. This self-downing has been described as 'psychological junk mail' and it affects students' ability to cope. There is a need to reframe the problem, looking at it realistically, and to help students to reframe these negatives into positives. It has been described as 'looking for the good in every situation'.

- *Goal setting and practising skills:* 'One small step' and 'a day at a time' would be the key phrases to use here. Setting easy-to-achieve targets and giving students opportunities to practise new patterns of behaviour in small steps would be beneficial as such actions can ensure success. Front-loaded reward systems are also important so that in the beginning students are frequently rewarded for modifying their behaviour.

- *Time-Out Card:* When students are finding it difficult to cope in sessions they can be issued with a 'Time-Out Card' for a limited period. The aim of this is to enable them to leave a lesson when conditions are such that they may do something they will regret. For example, another student may be winding them up so much that they might retaliate or the lecturer may say something that could cause them to explode. When a student feels that they may have to leave a lesson, because their anger may explode, they can show the card to their lecturer who will then let them leave the room to cool off. On leaving the session the student is expected to find a nominated member of staff who will then spend some time with them discussing the causes of their current problem and will give them various strategies to cope with this. The card is signed by the member of staff to show their arrival and departure time. In the ten years I have used this system students, lecturers and myself have found it a most useful way to reduce conflict. It has not been abused and students value and appreciate the time to reflect and have some space.

- *Peer mediation:* Involving a neutral third party to mediate and help settle conflict and disputes between students has been very successful in a number of institutions. This is a voluntary role and is not about making judgements as to who is right or wrong. The aim of the mediator is to help the disputants resolve their conflict. Mediators need to have:

  - good speaking and listening skills

  - the ability to heed the views, needs and feelings of disputants

  - the ability to find solutions, namely resolution skills.

  Peer mediation develops students' problem-solving ability and works because it empowers them to attempt to resolve conflict. It helps to develop a positive ethos where there is trust and open communication. There are also positive relationships. Former troublesome students have been found to be very effective mediators: as 'poacher turned gamekeeper'. They have first-hand experience of disputes and enjoy taking on the responsibility of settling conflict through negotiation.

- *Circle Time:* When students experience problems in relationships with other students or staff, resentments and anger may build over a period of time which – if not dealt with – can lead to serious repercussions for the student and others with whom they may come into contact. One technique that is used in many institutions to try to deal with such potential conflict is Circle Time, when students will sit in a circle and discuss their problems and successes. Clear protocols/rules must be established for the group to work. For example:

  - everyone has the right to express their feelings without being put down

  - only one person may speak at any time – sharing experiences and feelings openly is accepted by all group members

○ a positive atmosphere has to be maintained

○ the group leader thanks each member for their contributions.

Group members are encouraged to be supportive and 'the circle' offers advice on how students should react in the future. Where Circle Time is operated it can have a most beneficial effect on behaviour and on helping students to find solutions. I have seen this work very well in tutor sessions with students.

It is important when faced with conflict not to get sucked into an upward spiral. Some groups of students will frequently try to take control of the learning environment by testing us. By being calm, assertive, aware, firm and consistent we will be able to stay in control. When the going gets tough remember not to take the things angry students say personally: an angry child knows no boundaries and often young people will be testing what is acceptable behaviour in the safest environment they know – college.

Case Study

This Case Study concerns an accountancy lecturer working in a school with a group of 16-year-old students.

- The lecturer has to work with a group of 20 students for 36 weeks teaching them accountancy. They are taught in sessions of two hours duration.

- Accountancy is provided as one option among a number of option subjects available to the students.

- The school has had problems with 15 of the group who have displayed very troublesome and sometimes malicious behaviour.

- The same extreme behaviour has been displayed to other teachers in the school.

- The lecturer believes that no one else wanted to teach them so they were put altogether in this group.

- The learners making up the group are very resistant as they have difficulty in understanding the work and they are doing a course they did not wish to take.

1 In pairs, discuss the strategies you would use as the lecturer in this Case Study to manage the following more effectively:

Behaviour

_____

_____

Teaching and Learning

_____

_____

2   What interventions should the school and college undertake to improve the situation?

_____

_____

3   How could the school and college have ensured that these students were provided with a course that better met their needs?

_____

_____

Key points

- The reptilian part of the brain is concerned with survival: when it is triggered it senses danger and this leads to a fight, flight, freeze or flock response.

- This part of the brain can be triggered by deep-seated unresolved traumatic events in our lives.

- Students do not always have the emotional intelligence to decode the non-verbal and verbal communication used towards them.

- There are five phases to anger.

- There are clear physical signs that someone is about to become angry.

- Strategies lecturers can use are:

  - remain calm and give a clear instruction

  - be solution focused

  - avoid excessive eye contact

  - listen actively

  - develop a rapport.

- There are five anger styles.

- Students will 'act in' or 'act out' their anger.

- Support and strategies we can give students include:

  - dramatherapy

  - 'fire drills'

  - developing positive self-talk

  - giving students strategies to reduce stress – muscle relaxation, visualisation, anchoring, and breathing for relaxation.

CHAPTER 7

Managing difficult groups

We have all faced classes that are particularly challenging. It can sometimes appear as though all the worst-behaved students have been put together in the same group. Chris Watkins (1999) suggested that managing such groups in the classroom is 'perhaps the most complex and least understood situation on the planet'. It is the unpredictability and simultaneity of events that makes our job so challenging. Mathieson and Price (2002: 56) suggest that in managing behaviour in the classroom 'we are highly visible to all the other participants … which brings its own vulnerability'.

Why some groups will interact poorly with one another

In Chapter 1 we discussed the diverse range of backgrounds and experiences of learners in FE. When students come together in classes at the beginning of the academic year we can find groups of learners from a number of different schools being joined together with a variety of experiences in relation to the way their behaviour was managed in each institution. The students in each group will attempt to become the leader, the alpha male or alpha female, and this can cause problems and poor interactions between group members.

The same thing occurs with groups of 14- to16-year-old learners coming together in college for the first time. Some older learners will be returning to learning and can offer high levels of challenge to lecturers and to other group members.

Teaching mixed-age groups of learners can also lead to differences of opinion between older and younger learners. On top of this an increase in the numbers of students with additional needs in groups, sometimes without adequate support, can lead to problems between group members.

Stages in group formation

When a group of new students meets for the first time some inappropriate and immature behaviour can occur amongst members as the group tries to develop its own hierarchy and some learners attempt to become the dominant male or female in that group. Tuckman (1965) indicated that there were four clear stages in group formation:

- Forming – the group members are not sure about its structure.

- Storming – disagreements and conflicts occur between group members and the various subgroups that have formed.

- Norming – the group has become quite cohesive and more mature; rules have now been established.

- Conforming – the group works well on problem solving and conflicts are resolved.

By understanding these stages we are in a better position to manage these groups more effectively and to help accelerate the progress through the initial challenging stages. This can be done by using:

- appropriate induction activities

- team-building strategies

- a variety of co-operative learning strategies

- brain breaks which can help to develop a group rapport (examples of brain break activities can be found at www.brainbreaks.co.uk). When using brain breaks the whole group must be involved in a series of movements which will increase the electrical firings between left and right side of the brain. These also increase blood flow around the body and act as a mental intermission in a session. When doing this activity watch the whole group and spot who engages in it first and how many people follow them. If a number of the group do so that person is the rapport leader. Because of this no-one will engage in the activity until they do. It is essential that we use our own rapport building strategies with this leader so that we can get them onside and doing so will enable us to have a rapport with most of the group as a result.

Reflection on practice

Think of a challenging group you work with:

1   Identify the rapport leader (alpha student) in the group.

2   What strategies could you use to develop rapport with this learner to get them onside.

_____

_____

_____

Understanding the roles students may play in challenging groups

Key to successfully managing the behaviour of difficult groups is identifying the student roles within a group and using this to your advantage.

Students' key roles

- *Alpha male:* above-average intelligence, usually physically bigger than other group members.

- *Alpha female:* above-average intelligence, dressed in the latest fashions, uses sarcasm to control others.

- *Instigator:* starts trouble but usually gets away with it by being surreptitious.

- *Regulator/Questioner:* constantly interrupts, asking the same question in many different ways; note that these students can be very disruptive.

- *Deflector/Attention Diverter:* takes the heat off a student in trouble by deflecting the lecturer's attention using smart comments or minor misbehaviour.

- *Disruptor:* tactically aware: intervenes with the intention of disrupting when a lecturer is trying to regain control of a group.

- *Orchestrator:* co-ordinates much of the bad behaviour, acting as the 'conductor' for a 'symphony' of bad behaviour and 'orchestrating' outbursts from group to group.

- *Class Clown:* the class entertainer, who can be difficult to manage.

- *Fall Guy/Professional Victim:* male or female student who is happy to take the rap for things.

- *Challenger:* enjoys challenging the rules and any instructions given to them.

- *Invisible Person:* sometimes known as the 'radiator kid' because they will cling to a radiator, too afraid to move away from this zone of security.

- *Manipulator:* attempts to manipulate the students around them to do their work or gets them into trouble with staff.

- *Covert Operator:* appears pleasant but under the surface is undermining the lecturer's authority.

- *Constant Rule Breaker:* challenges rules and tests the boundaries.

- *Attention Seeker:* wants to be centre stage and under the spotlight at all times.

- *Sheep/Followers:* those students who blindly follow what others are doing.

- *Aggressive/Hostile Students:* those who act out their feelings in an aggressive manner.

Using a Neuro-Linguistic Programming approach to managing challenging groups of learners

When working with difficult groups it is essential that we identify the leaders in each group. Earlier in this chapter we looked at the importance of identifying the rapport leader in a group and using rapport building strategies to develop a connection with this learner. This is an example of a Neuro-Linguistic Programming (NLP) technique. NLP is about the way we communicate and how we behave. Using NLP can be highly effective when managing behaviour in the classroom. Mahony (2007: ix) suggests it is made up of three elements:

- building rapport and communicating with others

- gathering information about another person's view of the world

- promotion of behaviour-change strategies.

To demonstrate the power of NLP and the influence of body language in managing behaviour let us first examine *strategy elicitation*. This is where a member of staff picks out the leader in a group early on in each lesson, engages them in eye contact, and uses other non-verbal interactors. Elicitation is the technique for assisting someone else to move from one state to another. Through NLP researchers have tried to identify the strategies used by teachers who are successful in managing behaviour. Berry (2003) has discussed how research has attempted to identify the internal and external actions of successful staff and how they have tried to motivate other staff to replicate the same actions. Berry also suggested that successful staff can be very aware of the power of non-verbal communication. When settling groups they will identify a group of four or five influencers and leaders in the class and engage them in eye contact, giving them non-verbal cues that they want them to settle. These cues can also be effective in controlling poor behaviour. The sequence in which the member of staff looks at a group of four or five students is critical, as are the duration of the stare and the lecturer's position in the room. The sequence of non-verbal cues is important. Anyone observing this opening must replicate its sequence accurately. Any changes in sequence, duration, or type of non-verbal signals and they will not have the same level of success.

Alpha males and females

In the last section on understanding the roles students play we could see that the alpha males and females play an important role so it is important that we identify them as the leaders in our groups. These terms come from studies of animal behaviour which have shown that there is normally a dominant member in each pack. The term 'alpha male' was first used to describe aggressive American politicians in the 1950s.

- Typical alpha males will have a dress code that identifies them as belonging to a group or youth community and they are likely to be physically bigger than their peers and of above-average intelligence (see further Vizard, 2003). One parallel to this which you may have seen in the animal kingdom would be the baboon that sits at the top of the baboon rock at the local zoo.

- Alpha females will tend to show their traits from the age of 7 or 8. They will also tend to be sharper and brighter than their peers. They will be just as competitive as males and their bullying will be both subtle and cruel (see further Wyatt, 2002). Besag (2006) has suggested that girls are more effective bullies than boys and will use psychological warfare to dominate their victims. Alpha females will utilise psychological techniques to bully other females. Girls will rarely rely on violence but will instead choose to subtly undermine the confidence of others, an action which can be far more damaging and perhaps have lifelong effects on some victims. They will often use sarcastic stage whispers in order to undermine other girls in the group.

Working with disaffected groups of girls

Causes of disaffection

Increasing numbers of girls are displaying extreme and challenging behaviour in today's classrooms. Each of these groups is likely to be led by an alpha female. Dr Carolyn Jackson, at the Department for Education Research at Lancaster University (see Jackson, 2004), found in a survey of girls in the north of England that there was an increase in ladette behaviour, with a growing number of teenage girls becoming loud and rowdy, swearing and fighting a lot, and being assertive. Her report confirmed these aspects by stating that the research had found that 'Within the classroom environment "ladettes" are portrayed by fellow pupils as hard, loud, disruptive, rude to teachers, mildly aggressive to some other pupils and frequently swearing ... Teachers also suggest that "ladettes" are aggressively assertive, "in your face" and arrogant'.

According to the British Association of Anger Management (Eccles, 2010) girls are copying some aspects of aggressive male behaviour. The number of teenage girls who will lash out and are physically aggressive has increased dramatically. Mike Fisher, an anger management psychotherapist (Eccles, 2010), has suggested that there is a strong link between binge drinking amongst young girls and their physical aggression. He has also suggested that other potential triggers for anger include family breakdown, bullying and premature sexualisation.

Portrayals of girls in the media in soaps, and in particular on reality television shows, promote competitiveness and often a need to eliminate competitors. Adverts and products also often encourage early sexualisation and experimentation. In addition, social networking sites can have a negative impact on girls' behaviour. Ladette culture also frowns upon educational achievement and instead promotes girls becoming streetwise. The influence of gangs can mean a pack mentality and girls forced to do extreme things to ensure their membership. Managing groups of girls who are disaffected and display ladette behaviour can be extremely challenging for lecturers.

Types of bullying that can occur in groups of girls

One control mechanism that groups of girls use is psychological techniques to dominate a victim. If a victim transgresses fashion, friendship or dating codes then the consequences can be profound. The bullying that occurs can be extremely damaging and can have lifelong effects. Professor Helen Cowie suggests that gangs of girls can make someone's life hell. They work together in a group which is from where their strength will come. Girls will be involved in more covert types of bullying, using nasty looks, catty comments, or excluding behaviour. Some of the nasty tricks employed can include:

- making a victim drop her old friends if she wants to join the in-group and then excluding her anyway

- not issuing a victim with a party invitation, or encouraging her to organise a party and then ensuring no one turns up

- stealing a victim's workbook from the homework pile and hiding it

- starting rumours about a victim.

Friendship appears to be more important to girls than academic success. They will fear being isolated if they are pushed out of a friendship group. According to information presented to a House of Commons Education Select Committee, girls will resort to using 'rumour-mongering and "social isolation"' to control their victims. David Moore (2006), a senior Ofsted inspector, highlighted how non-verbal communication could prove to be a powerful weapon: for example, a group of girls will walk up to another girl who thinks they are all friends and then simply walk away, thereby isolating her and leaving her publicly humiliated. Girls will also typically exclude others from their circle by employing cruel words and deviously back-stabbing others. They can be obsessed by the consumer culture, with its emphasis on clothes and looks. Such girls will be supremely confident.

Interventions that work with bullying behaviour in groups of girls

In the classroom we need to use strategies to break up the power base of such groups of aggressive girls, as indeed we must do with other groups of students. A group of ladettes will get their strength from acting as a group and therefore they are likely to have a leader – the alpha female. She will be controlling and loud and will use sarcasm and stage whispers to isolate others. She will try to assemble her group close to her in lessons. I will often try to break up such groups by re-arranging the class. To do this I will sometimes give out cards numbered 1 to 5 and place students together with those who have the same number. This immediately breaks up the power base and will isolate the alpha female and her other group members. If the cluster is dispersed it is less likely that it will be effective.

Early intervention strategies need to occur when we identify any instances of bullying. The promotion of bystanders' importance in bullying incidents is central to reducing this: 'Give the bystanders the skills to know how to respond and stop the violence in a safe way' advises Rita Adair, an educational psychologist with the Anti-Bullying Alliance (www.anti-bullyingalliance.org.uk). It is entirely possible to change a ringleader's actions by empowering those around her. The chief bully, or 'Queen Bee', needs the laughter and attention of the crowd. If the hangers-on refuse to condone her behaviour, she will be left isolated. One way to do this is to discuss the different levels of culpability with the class. Who is really to blame for this: the main bully, her sidekicks, those who fan the flames, or the seemingly innocent bystanders? By asking these questions the class will realise that bullying is everyone's responsibility.

Using work by kidscape (www.kidscape.co.uk) with victims in order to empower them is worthwhile here. There are also other programmes that can be used with groups of girls to help them reflect on what is occurring and, through role plays, to develop more positive relationships. Initially supporting the victims of bullying is key. Many institutions use 'The Virginia Satir's Daily Temperature Reading' and deliver this as Circle Time lessons, where groups will consider key areas including appreciation, new information, puzzles, complaints, and their wishes, hopes and dreams in order to develop positive relationships. Some institutions made use of 'The Scary Guy', an American who has a very clear message on bullying and the way to develop a community ethos where bullying will not occur (www.thescaryguy.com). Other colleges have set up a range of diversionary activities to support the victims of bullying.

Reflection on practice

A group of five girls in an all girl Fashion Design group have started to pick on another girl and begun to spread malicious rumours about her being promiscuous which are unfounded and untrue. They have also started talking about the girl within her earshot in the learning environment using stage whispers. They are now encouraging other students to ignore her and are trying very hard to isolate her. In addition they have also started making negative comments about her on social networking sites. In pairs, discuss which strategies you would use to manage this student.

_____

_____

_____

Cyber bullying and online safety

New communications technology and the internet have given students numerous ways in which to socialise, communicate, and connect with others. Technology and its applications are rapidly changing and so it is extremely difficult to ensure we are keeping up to date with some of the negative things that can occur through use of it. Cyber bullying is a real concern and its impact is more devastating due to its 24/7 nature. It can make students feel helpless, sad, frustrated and socially anxious. It is also a significant problem amongst British children, with over 20 per cent reporting aggressive and unpleasant behaviour online. Such bullying can occur through:

- abusive texts

- negative use of social networking sites

- offensive and harassing emails often from dummy accounts

- blogs being set up which aim to spread false rumours

- websites being set up that are defamatory.

The internet can be a paradise for bullies as they can be extremely hurtful to their victims and yet remain anonymous. No student should feel that they have to face and deal with cyber bullying alone. However, there is no single solution to the problem. To help reduce the risk of cyber bullying and to promote online safety, colleges should:

- produce a clear policy and guidance on the safe and acceptable use of communication technology

- have clear statements relating to cyber bullying and how it will be dealt with by the college: this should be linked to an anti-bullying policy

- encourage all staff to be vigilant for signs of cyber bullying

- have clear systems for recording any incidents and actions

- give students a clear indication of who they can report cases to within a college: clear advice is given at www.childnet.com/digizen on where they can receive help and support externally

- ask students to sign a contract listing the terms and conditions for their responsible use of email and the internet

- educate students via induction programmes about the potential risks and what they should do if any problems arise: they must also promote 'netiquette' and e-safety

- keep the filtering and restricting access software up to date

- urge students to realise that CEOP (the Child Exploitation and Online Protection Centre: www.ceop.police.uk) is a key organisation which can be used to enable them to report online abuse. It has substantial resources on issues such as cyber bullying through to grooming by child sex offenders. The issue of 'sexting' is also covered – namely where young people will take indecent images which will then be circulated to a wider audience. Some learners can put themselves at risk by daring each other to send inappropriate images to students of the opposite sex

- be aware of the need to give advice and guidance on chatroom safety and this is provided at the following website: www.chatdanger.com

Specific advice to students could include the following:

- If they receive abusive or obscene texts or video messages they should contact their mobile service provider.

- If abusive emails and inappropriate sites are being uploaded which are defamatory they should report this to the Internet Service Provider (ISP). They will have an Acceptable Usage Policy (AUP) that includes their terms and conditions. If they go to www.bullying.co.uk they will get advice on how to find out further details on the possible owner of a website. It is important students do not reply to this kind of email. Also it may be useful for them to identify the sender by right clicking the mouse over the email which will show them its origin. If serious they should make a copy of the offending email – this could be saved or printed out using print screen.

Another useful resource area on the topic of cyber bullying is www.kidscape.org.uk

Working with disaffected groups of males

In secondary schools males are four times more likely than girls to be excluded from school; 83 per cent of all secondary exclusions involve boys (Osler et al., 2002). The most difficult groups of male students can offer high levels of challenge and are often led by an alpha male. To them peer group influences are very important. They can also work together as a group in class and have a very destructive effect. Males enjoy the 'instant gratification' they can get from the response of lecturers and fellow students when they misbehave. Many students we work with will be 'eager to please', but this is not the case with this group.

The following strategies can help reduce the effect of this group:

- Position male and female students in mixed seating arrangements.

- Males enjoy sociable learning, so organise them to work in groups/pairs that do not include other students from their friendship groups.

- Engage male students in active learning. Use time-limited tasks where learners have to transfer their learning from one medium to another (for example, going from a video/play to an oral report). In many classrooms male students will be expected to learn passively.

- Introduce a trial and error speculative approach to learning. This is an experimental approach in which learners understand that it is acceptable to make mistakes.

- Be aware that males have a low boredom threshold and shorter attention span, so try to plan a larger number of shorter tasks.

- Adopt a clear structure for their work. Have established protocols for various activities.

- Remember that male students may only be able to do one thing at a time and plan activities accordingly.

- Recognise that among males learning is not seen as 'cool'. Males do not like to stand out and so they will underachieve. They also like to gain notoriety through poor behaviour. Institutions often perpetuate this situation by continuing to tolerate an 'anti-boffin culture'.

Strategies to use with difficult groups

When faced with poor behaviours in a challenging group we need to become Miss Marple or Hercule Poirot and try to play the detective. Ask yourself why is this behaviour happening with me in this specific setting? Then look at the antecedents to that behaviour. Try to identify the triggers to the behaviour and identify how the behaviour manifested itself. In addition attempt to identify the consequence or pay-off for the student. If we reflect on poor behaviour in this way we can develop successful strategies to manage that behaviour. Note that Learning Support Assistants may be able to answer all of the above fairly easily. They could also be able to recommend a solution-focused approach for a particular student and pinpoint when their poor behaviour is least likely to occur and the sorts of strategies used by that member of staff.

More general strategies we can use include the following.

- Many students are testing the boundaries to see how far they may be able to go. To stay in control you will need to give all learners a structure, a routine, and firm boundaries.

- You should have some flexibility in your repertoire and thus be able to make a sudden change in your manner when necessary.

- It is important to make it difficult for students to read you – being somewhat unpredictable can be an asset.

- Early intervention is essential by predicting which poor behaviours are likely to occur before they even start.

- It is vital to have blitzes on particular areas of poor behaviour throughout the year.

Do not perceive poor behaviour as a personal attack. This would be very unlikely and most often a student will be experimenting to learn how to behave appropriately by testing the boundaries in a safe environment. In addition remember that some students will have their bad behaviour so deeply ingrained in them, very often as a survival strategy in their lives outside college, that they will not even be aware of the fact they are behaving badly. Think about how we drive a car for example. Our driving skills are so deeply ingrained in us that we do not need to think about what we are doing at a conscious level. Something similar may well be happening with students who are demonstrating challenging behaviour in the classroom.

Many students can also give the appearance of being supremely confident when in fact they have low self-esteem and are struggling to gain the recognition of their peers. Many can become involved in poor behaviour with others in order to gain plaudits from their peer group. Michael Marland (2001) has suggested that these students 'get caught up in what is called "the prison of the peer groups" – they pretend they are toughly "being themselves", but actually they have been cast in the role of troublemakers, happily taken the casting, and are seeking the satisfaction of others, admiring their troublesome role'.

Strategies to use with groups that interact poorly with one another

Poor interpersonal relationships between students in a particular class may often lead to discipline problems for lecturers. Endless disputes amongst learners can make such a group very difficult to teach and also have a debilitating effect on staff. With such groups the following strategies may be useful:

- Hold meetings for staff who normally have to teach the group.

- Identify the various types of poor behaviour and how the group is dysfunctional.

- Select five examples of poor behaviour and reach an agreement on three ways you will deal with each behaviour.

- Remember that consistency is key: if students experience a consistent approach then there will be a reduction in poor behaviour. (For this you could employ the Consistency Model exercise used in Chapter 8.)

- Develop a rewards system. Identify the types of poor behaviour everyone would like to reduce. For example, when dealing with a group in which students are making inappropriate comments to one another:

○ Inform students that you will be keeping a tally of negative and positive comments during the lesson.

○ Set the targets that you want them to achieve in relation to the ratio of positive to negative comments.

○ Also give them examples of some positive comments that they can make to each other.

○ If these targets are achieved issue a reward for the group.

○ If any students attempt to sabotage the system have a punishment system in place – for example, isolation/withdrawal.

Sometimes it may be necessary to develop a series of activities in order to encourage greater co-operation and assist with the socialisation amongst group members. These activities could improve positivity and cohesion amongst classes. The activities would need to be of a team-building nature, with some offering a high level of challenge. A number of these would be needed to cover a wide variety of personal skills. The emphasis would be on:

- total group involvement

- constructive communication

- positive co-operation

- good discipline and behaviour

- sensible use of personal skills within groups

- punctuality.

As lecturers, when faced with groups such as these, we can tend to become very negative: we will generalise and say that they are out of control when they are not. With such groups there will be times that are less bad. Try to remember these. Always attempt to anticipate the bad behaviour. And when groups are badly behaved, use this as a learning experience. Sometimes changing the way you organise a group for activities can improve their behaviour.

Reflection on practice

1   With a partner discuss and list types of inappropriate behaviours that are presented by the difficult and challenging groups you teach.

_____
_____
_____
_____
_____
_____

(a) Are any of these behaviours unique to younger aged groups of learners? If so, place a letter Y next to those behaviours on your list.

(b) Are any of these behaviours unique to older learners (adult groups)? If so, place a letter A next to those behaviours on your list.

(c) Discuss any specific strategies from the information given in this chapter and from your own knowledge which would be helpful to use with groups of older learners/adult groups. List these below.

_____
_____
_____
_____
_____
_____

Case Study: Developing positive working relationships in a Building and Construction practical area

At college a lecturer had organised his workshop in a particularly successful way. During the day he had two groups of 14- to 16-year-old learners from two schools arriving at staggered times. The first group would arrive at 9am, the next at 10am. There was a clear routine for each group to follow. On arriving they would assemble in a small classroom area attached to the practical area. Here the students would chat with the lecturer as tasks for the session were allocated. Relationships were excellent and the lecturer would even gave up some of his time to referee the students in a football match at lunchtime. Students would then put on their protective clothing, boots and goggles. Each group were experiencing tiling, plastering and bricklaying and some elementary carpentry on a rotating programme. Therefore at any one time there would be groups of students involved in four separate activities in that one room. When the second group arrived the same routine would be followed. It was interesting to note that these students would then also integrate well with peers from other schools in the same workshop area. At the end of the session following their clearing up and changing, students gathered together in the classroom area for a debrief and to help plan for the next session.

This session, with difficult and challenging students, worked well because of the structure, organisation and routine established by the lecturer. A lot also depended on the good relationship set up by the lecturer during the establishment phase.

Stimulating activities to engage learners in challenging groups

With the current emphasis on personalised learning, it is necessary to understand learners' style diversity so that we can develop a range of activities that will match their individual learning profiles. Each learner will have a unique profile. Barbara Prashnig (2006) developed Learning Style Analysis for Learners, whereby students would complete questionnaires that looked at issues such as hemispheric dominance, sensory preference, brain processing, thinking style, the environments in which they worked best – relating to light, sound and temperature – and their social group preference, from operating alone to team working. Another part of this profile could include Howard Gardner's Multiple Intelligences (Gardner and Hatch, 1989) where every individual has a balance of intelligences – these include interpersonal, intrapersonal, linguistic, mathematic and logical, visual and spatial, kinaesthetic, musical and naturalist. Using the Learning Style Analysis, both an individual and group profile can be produced.

The best way to motivate learners and help them learn information is to get them actively involved. The most effective way to achieve retention of learning is to ensure young people practise by doing, and especially where they can teach others and make immediate use of their learning. Using these two approaches will give 75 per cent and 90 per cent average retention rates respectively, according to George (1995).

Co-operative learning strategies

Co-operative learning strategies require students to work with each other as they learn. The lesson is structured so that students will have a vested interest in each other's learning as well as their own. This approach can be very challenging for learners but it is highly effective academically and socially.

Jigsaw techniques

The jigsaw technique is one approach to developing co-operative learning. Students are divided into groups of five and each group discusses five aspects of a particular topic. A Catering lecturer in one college has used this approach to get students to think about ways of cooking five different meats – such as turkey, chicken, beef, lamb and pork. One member in each group is responsible for the approach to cooking one of the categories of meat. After a short period students will re-group into groups relating to the meat they discussed – for example, all the 'beefs' will go together. They will then become a specialist group and come up with the best three ways to cook their meat. Each group will in turn prepare a report to give to the others. A variation on this would be to have each group specialising in ways to cook one meat. Then students would be re-grouped so that one member from the beef group joined one member each from the lamb, pork, turkey and chicken groups. Each person would then have to present the various ways decided on to cook their meat to the rest of the group.

Another way to use this approach is to set up five resource areas in a room to do with a single topic: for example, internet access, posters, book resources, audio/video/DVD and an expert. Students in groups of five will allocate one student in each group to visit one area. They will then return having collected key information that they will feed back to other members of their group.

There are many strengths to this approach and these include:

- high levels of challenge including individual accountability

- greater involvement for group members – positive interdependence

- empowerment

- peer teaching

- task-based/learning by doing

- active learning

- increased motivation

- social skills development

- a higher level of reasoning

- members being allowed to assess the work of their peers.

Co-operative learning helps to create a positive climate for learning in which social skills are developed and students can learn to accept and give constructive feedback.

Some support strategies that could be used with difficult groups include the following:

- Attaching students to a mentor or 'charismatic hero'. Some colleges will attach senior staff to these students to guide them.

- Having line managers drop in on a lesson involving badly behaving groups and maintaining a high profile in lesson time.

- Using adults external to the college as mentors. This could involve using intergenerational schemes, people from business, sportsmen and women, engineers, or people from the world of music, including DJs.

- Engaging disaffected students in a student-run radio station, writing a daily news sheet including news, quizzes and music pages to be used by all students at registration.

- Increasing motivation through schemes linking sporting successes with achievement in the classroom.

- Involving students in contemporary drama, which engages them in discussing key issues and allows them a safe framework for experimenting with concepts and ideas.

- Giving these students a whole range of responsibilities.

Some other strategies that could be adopted include the following:

- Adopt a secret student strategy – with groups and in particular difficult groups, get the students involved in a secret student strategy. Get a group to decide a reward that they would like each week or half-term. The group will receive this reward if there is a 75 per cent success rate in a secret student achieving three targets. These targets are agreed with the group initially. In each session one student is selected by the lecturer to be the secret student (the student or group is not told that they are the secret student). If they achieve their three targets they are told that they were the secret student and have been successful in achieving their targets. If they were not successful the group are told that they have been unsuccessful and have not achieved their target. However the secret student is not identified. This strategy can have a significant impact on modifying the behaviour of a group.

- Split up troublesome groups. Put names in a pot and have a raffle to select seats.

- Involve the most challenging students as group leaders, helpers and monitors.

- In groups, give rewards to a group if they are successful at a task. Misbehaviour by any member of the group results in no reward.

- Use stealth tactics. Introduce individual tasks that will divert students so that they do not realise they have been split up.

- Ensure they have work that they can cope with, be successful with, and of which they can be proud.

- Have short, structured activities that allow for instant gratification.

- Establish ground rules ensuring group ownership and responsibility.

- Include differentiated activities with competitions and rewards.

- Try to develop a positive group identity.

Influence of gangs and youth communities

There is a rising influence of gangs and youth communities which is having a significant impact on behaviour in the college environment. Over 5 per cent of students will be in or on the fringes of gang culture.

Reasons for membership

- Family breakdowns have led to students replacing parental and family role models with gang members for support.

- Gangs offer security and a sense of identity and belonging which helps to raise student self-esteem.

- Push factors which cause students to join gangs mean that they avoid the negatives of:

  - loneliness

  - bullying

  - victimisation

  - isolation

  - boredom.

- Pull factors or positive factors which cause students to join gangs mean:

  - the gang is your group of friends and a second family

  - there is protection from other gangs and threats of violence

  - they have a role and a status

  - security and support can be found

  - they have a sense of identity

  - peers will watch your back

  - their emotional needs are met by the gang membership.

Indication of gang membership

Some of the following would be an indication of gang membership:

- Tags/graffiti symbols on books and college possessions – graffiti on buildings will sometimes be crossed out by rival gangs.

- Signs of territorial allegiance – turf wars. There can be a clear marking of boundaries by trophies or graffiti.

- Wearing similar items of clothing to others in their group – special colours, bandanas, hats, hoodies or items of jewellery (bling).

- Wearing clothes to protect against weapons – for example, knives.

- The sudden acquisition of expensive items.

- Secretive behaviour – suspicious use of mobiles and the internet. This may also include profiles on networking sites such as Bebo and My Space.

- The use of hand and other signals.

- The use of a restricted code language – for example, nicknames in order to exclude others (breddrin, coz, jeezie, wyfie, my boys). Use of extremist language.

- A rise in student absence/absconding during the day.

- Carrying weapons (for self-protection) and making threats of violence.

- Specific groupings of students – for example, ethnicity-based in combination with some of the other indicators given in this section.

- Linking up with outsiders during the college day.

- Sudden changes in friendship groups.

- Over-sexualised language and behaviour. Gangs make girls subservient and submissive and girls in gangs are sexually exploited.

Safeguarding issues

Given the number of younger learners now involved in colleges, the issues on safeguarding raised in general safeguarding guidelines (DfES, 2006) and in those concerned with safeguarding children and young people who may be affected by gang activity (DCSF/Home Office, 2010) should be carefully considered. There is a clear emphasis here that safeguarding in relation to gangs should be preventative and responsive. It should focus on those who are in gangs and at risk of harm, as well as addressing the risk factors of other young people being drawn into gangs in the future. It is clear that early intervention is essential to help young people avoid falling into the downward spiral of violence, substance abuse and criminal behaviour that is associated with membership of some gangs. Gang members will begin offending in their early teens (the average age for a first conviction is 15 years old).

The issue of safeguarding also relates to the use of cyber space and gang members utilising internet chatrooms to bully people into joining gangs. Carrying and using weapons such as knives is a priority issue. Multi-agency working is a key way of ensuring support and safeguarding our learners which involves education, social care, health, welfare, protection, the police, crime prevention, prisons, the probation service and the voluntary and community sectors working together.

Reflection on practice

1 In groups of five spend five minutes having a thought shower on how gangs and youth communities may be impacting on the behaviour of students in your learning environments. You will need one person recording the comments on flipchart paper.

2 Discuss any effective strategies you could use to overcome this challenge. List your Top Ten ideas on flipchart paper.

3 Display the findings from all groups and then discuss what the college needs to do to negate the more negative aspects of gang culture.

Prevention

Classroom strategies

- Develop a positive group identity, for example by using 'The Virginia Satir's Daily Temperature Reading' (referred to earlier in the chapter).

- Use co-operative learning approaches to re-arrange clusters of gang members in the classroom.

- Use dramatherapy and role play to deal with gang-related issues.

- Remember that gang-related issues need to be central to areas of the curriculum. This will:

  ○ promote community cohesion

  ○ discuss issues of diversity

  ○ illustrate how to manage risk and resolve conflict

  ○ resist negative pressure

  ○ promote safe and healthy behaviours.

- Use mentoring to divert at-risk students towards safer activities at times of a high risk of gang involvement.

- Promote a more attractive brand than gangs – use sport, enterprise and music to do this.

Skills development

Students need to learn how to:

- use clear communication in difficult situations

- understand how to manage their anger

- recognise anger in others and learn how to calm them

- resolve conflicts and gain respect for others

- fully understand the consequences of fighting

- set goals and behave with responsibility

- avoid drugs and become able to resist peer pressure.

Diversionary strategies

A number of diversionary strategies will be organised by external groups, although college facilities could be used for some of these.

- Late-night sports activities including midnight sports such as basketball and soccer.

- The use of street pastors who work towards engaging young people on the street, particularly those who feel marginalised and excluded.

- The Boston Miracle Scheme in Glasgow run by the Violence Reduction Unit. Gang members meet with police and church leaders. Those who accept jobs counselling and support roles are given reduced sentences. The scheme invites five members from the 55 recognised gangs in Glasgow. As a result of this initiative there has been a reduction in violent crime of 50 per cent in two years.

Organisations and support

- To enable colleges to support students there needs to be appropriate professional development for staff on the topic. Staff need to be able to recognise the signs of gang membership, as well as be aware of the legal powers and interventions that are available.

- Good links with external agencies are key here so that appropriate intelligence can be gathered that may help interventions to occur at an early stage.

- Developing opportunities for confidential support in colleges must also include psychological support.

- External groups can be used to help support a safe exit strategy for those students who wish to leave gangs.

- The involvement of parents and family is important. The document *Gangs: You and Your Child* (Home Office, 2010) is particularly useful for this.

- Safer Cities is run by Metropolitan Black Police Association and is aimed at young people living in poor communities. It helps to tackle gang culture by encouraging them to become community leaders.

- The Tackling Knives and Serious Youth Violence Action Programme (TKAP) exists in 16 police force areas to enable 13- to 24-year-olds to become engaged in positive activities.

- LEAP is a charity which addresses youth conflict, helping young people to find causes and creative approaches as solutions to conflict. The work done does not aim to portray gangs as bad but focuses instead on the consequences of certain actions. It also involves practical activities which include reflection and skills development. The four main areas covered are:

  ○ safety and danger

  ○ space and territory

  ○ status and reputation

  ○ enemies and revenge.

  For more information go to www.leaplinx.com

Case Study – A successful intervention to support learners at risk through gang involvement

In one particular institution fighting between groups was common. The gangs were divided by ethnic origin and students would bring in weapons to protect themselves. Fights would often start because of a look or students 'bad-mouthing' one another. The students were taken away on a residential trip, initially with each group going separately and then as a combined unit. It was the first time the group members had been able to talk about how they felt. The activities, using LEAP materials and facilitators, involved learning how to resolve conflicts and handle situations. They also learnt that there were no good or bad choices but there were costs to behaving in a particular way. Activities included:

- A Conflict Map.

  - Students were asked to draw a map of their area and show where conflicts were likely to occur, when they occurred, and who was likely to be involved.

  - They were asked to relate conflicts to particular locations.

  - They were asked to show where they felt safe – this involved very few locations.

  - Students examined the Red Flag – looking at what made them angry in those locations.

- Gamble of Revenge – students used dice to show how the cycle of violence could escalate.

- FIDO – Fact, Interpretation, Decision and Outcome – students used this to illustrate how a disrespectful look was a matter of opinion and a violent response could lead to a court appearance.

As a result of the work of LEAP, relationships across the ethnic groups have been transformed. Previously students were making bad choices. Now they are building their self-respect and self-esteem.

Key points

- Have an inbuilt flexibility to your repertoire.

- Early interventions are essential.

- Play the detective – why is a group or an individual being difficult? Look for triggers and pay offs.

- Note the stages in group formation – forming, storming, norming and conforming.

- Use brain breaks to develop a group rapport and to get the rapport leader onside.

(Continued)

(Continued)

- Identify the various roles played by group members.

- Identify the alpha males and females and use strategy elicitation.

- When working with disaffected groups of girls be aware of the psychological techniques some girls will use in bullying and utilise bystanders to modify their behaviour.

- Recognise the impact of cyber bullying and the importance of online safety.

- Use a range of strategies, including those mentioned in this chapter.

- With groups that do not relate well to one another, use behaviour modification strategies – set small-scale targets for improvement and reward these when achieved.

- Use group building activities regularly.

- Adopt co-operative learning strategies.

- Use the range of starter activities and brain break strategies outlined.

- Remember to use the secret student strategy.

- In relation to gangs be aware of:

  - the reasons for membership

  - the push and pull factors

  - the ways to identify gang membership

  - safeguarding issues

  - preventative strategies including skills development and support.

CHAPTER 8

Establishing a consistent approach

The importance of consistency

It is essential that when managing individuals and groups of students we are consistent in our responses and how we manage their behaviour. Students respond well when they know exactly where they stand with each member of staff – they respect firm boundaries. It is also important that there is a consistent approach amongst all staff on how key behaviours are managed. If you track a student from lesson to lesson it will be interesting to note the lack of consistency in the management of behaviour from room to room. All staff, including support staff, have an important role to play in managing behaviour. One area that is often ignored is the management of behaviour outside the classroom, in corridors in communal areas and outside the building. It is essential that all staff are involved in the management of behaviour in these areas, because if poor behaviour is ignored here it will have a negative impact on student behaviour in the classroom.

Key areas of consistency are as follows:

- We need to model emotional consistency.

- We must be very consistent in our responses to situations.

- We must be consistent in the language we use in key situations.

- We must also be consistent in the way we manage behaviour outside the classroom.

- We need to develop consistent environments with appropriate peripheral learning displays, give consistent visual messages on behaviour expectations, and develop behaviour management displays in each room.

Reflection on practice – developing a Consistency Model

To develop a consistent approach in staff teams I often use this exercise. In your group elect someone to lead the activity. They should then:

1   Ask staff to identify five types of poor behaviour presented by groups of students.

2   Choose five different colours of paper and allocate one to each of these behaviours.

3   Divide staff into groups of five with each group member being given one of the five different coloured pieces of paper.

4   Have each group identify two strategies to use with each behaviour, with the person holding the relevant coloured piece of paper representing that behaviour listing two agreed strategies.

5   Form specialist colour groups after 15 minutes, whereby staff with the same coloured piece of paper will assemble together and come up with the five best strategies to deal with their specialist behaviour.

6   Place the five best strategies for each of the five behaviours on one side of a sheet of A4 paper as a Consistency Model Chart: staff will then be expected to apply any of these strategies, but only these strategies, when faced with the listed challenging behaviours.

To help in the development of the Consistency Model described above, the remainder of this chapter lists a range of different challenging behaviours that students display and offers various strategies you may like to use for managing these.

Poor timekeeping/late arrival in class

We must have a consistent approach to managing student lateness:

- During the induction phase we need to establish a clear agreement on our expectations for punctuality. We must emphasise to learners the likely outcome of their lateness in the work setting (for example, verbal and written warnings).

- We must quickly ask the reason for lateness and make it clear we will deal with this later. We need to minimise any disruption to the class and when appropriate ask that student to fill in a grid with the reason for their late arrival.

  - At an appropriate moment issue them with a piece of paper divided into six squares.

  - Ask them to fill in one square with the following information – date, subject, number of minutes late, reason and signature.

- ○ On the sixth occasion photocopy the sheet, retain one copy and hand the other one on to the Pastoral Co-ordinator.

  ○ Arrange for them to send a copy of the sheet home. Most students will say they do not care if their parents are informed, but they will – 'doesn't care ... really does care!'

- With groups of students 'showboating' by making a grand late entry, we must wrong foot them by not allowing them to disrupt the lesson. In this instance we can ask them to wait outside or get them to settle in their seats quickly.

- We need to have a variety of seats reserved for latecomers scattered around the room. We must ensure these are in low profile areas and perhaps in locations where students would lose their street credibility if they had to sit there.

- We must ensure students make up for lost time.

- We should issue positive rewards to those students who arrive on time.

- We should utilise positive peripheral learning notices (for example, 'Thank you for arriving punctually').

- Tutors/mentors/pastoral care staff should set reduction targets with those students who are persistently late.

Use of mobiles and other electronic devices

- Clear guidance on this needs to be given in college policy and supported by notices in each learning area. The consequences of using mobiles and other electronic devices also need to be made clear. These should form part of the college contract as well.

- It is essential that there is a consistent application of this policy by all staff.

- In some institutions the following guidelines work well:

  ○ Students switch off their mobiles at the beginning of lessons and these are placed on the desk in front of them. The session will not begin until this has been accomplished by all students. Peer pressure from those students wanting the lesson to start will ensure compliance.

  ○ If phones are used they will be securely stored in an envelope with the student's name on it until the agreed collection time.

- We can use a 'no mobile phone use' as one of the criteria for assessing the 'secret student' (refer to Chapter 7).

- We can log any incidents of mis-use of mobiles and electronic devices and send these to the relevant tutors.

Reluctance to participate

- Find out reasons why – there may be an issue relating to additional needs or a student not fully understanding the work. Provide or arrange necessary support. Use Prashnig's Unique Learner Profile Work (see Chapter 7).

- Break the work down into manageable chunks and set short-term targets. Give rewards when tasks are completed. Students can then enjoy instant gratification.

- Use co-operative learning strategies so learners work in groups and are less likely to let down their peers.

- Develop buddying where a student works with another student with higher levels of motivation.

- Develop a variety of tasks which are time limited, practical and fun. Introduce an element of competition where possible.

- Use lots of praise and encouragement.

Lack of equipment including professional clothing and protective gear

- At the start of lessons allow students 30 seconds to sort out any lack of equipment, otherwise they will be given a first strike and 30 seconds' detention.

- Keep an emergency stock of spare equipment. If a pen is forgotten give the student a green ink biro. It is then easy to keep track of the number of times a pen has been forgotten when you look through their work. Also remember that green ink does not give them any street credibility.

- Trade your pen for a piece of their equipment, thereby you ensure its safe return.

- Set up 'Points make Prizes' where students will lose points for forgetting equipment. The student with the most points in class at the end of the week/term wins a prize.

- Include an agreement on equipment in a student contract.

- Develop techniques to help students remember, for example using checklists.

- Remember that it is difficult to provide alternative items of professional clothing (for example, protective and safety gear like boots and goggles) because of Health and Safety as well as hygiene. Wherever possible hold back a small stock of some items for students to use. Ask a tutor/mentor to develop some ways whereby students can more easily remember to bring items.

- In vocational areas develop the mindset of the world of work. Ultimately you would lose your job if you didn't bring in your professional equipment/tools/protective gear. There would also be a stigma attached to forgetting things.

Inappropriate use of the internet

This is a key issue with inappropriate sites being accessed in class either on the college network or by students using their mobile phones. Insisting on mobiles being switched off and visible on everyone's desk will remove one potential access point. In relation to accessing inappropriate sites on a college network:

- All students should sign the terms and conditions for responsible use of the internet in college which must include those sites which should not be visited. If these are accessed there should be clear sanctions listed in the agreement.

- Up-to-date filtering and restricting software should be used to stop access to inappropriate sites.

- Monitoring software should be used to identify if any student has managed to circumvent these blocks. This will mean that a member of staff can take appropriate action. In one college a monitoring team arrives to challenge students about the inappropriate sites they have visited (with a printout of the evidence). Informing parents, as well as sanctioning students, works well.

Poor corridor behaviour

If corridor behaviour is not managed appropriately this can have an impact in the classroom. Some lecturers find moving along corridors quite intimidating. Often students will be challenging in communal areas and aspects of gang culture (discussed in Chapter 7) can be more obvious in corridor areas.

- It is essential that all staff deal with poor behaviour in corridors and spaces outside their classrooms in a consistent manner.

- A staff presence is needed in key areas such as pinch points (where corridors narrow) or at cross-over points at times of student movement.

- Try to engage in conversation and be positive – catch 'em being good.

- When walking around the site all staff need to do so with confidence, choosing their positioning in corridors carefully and using body language techniques such as those mentioned earlier, including the look, non-verbal cues and silence, to indicate their disapproval and whilst waiting for student compliance. You will need to build a reputation, a credibility by proxy.

- If issuing an instruction use single command words and speak at the lower end of your two-octave vocal range.

- Beware of entrapment or 'chase-me' behaviours which will be done purely in order to set you up. Some tactical ignoring may be appropriate here.

- Try to avoid situations where you must deal with a student in front of a large group of their peers. The oxygen of publicity that this generates for them could result in a negative outcome. Move to a different location that is away from the peer group to discuss an issue.

Low-level disturbance

- Move closer to noisy students. Stand inside their 46cm space bubble and ask about their work rather than acknowledge the disturbance.

- If a student is fiddling with an object state that the item/equipment should be put away or it will be kept by you until the end of the lesson. Keep this exchange friendly. Remove the item if necessary.

- Use non-verbal signals to reduce any disturbance (for example, fingers to lips).

- Refer to the disturbance behaviour but still carry on with the session. Do not allow students' actions to disrupt your session.

- Pause momentarily and look directly at the student, but say nothing.

- Use a positive attention getter (for example, a whistle or bell) to get their attention. You could also develop a mutual cue when you want the group to come together (for example, you clap and they clap back).

Swearing

- Make the class rules and consequences for swearing clear at the beginning of the year.

- Help students to understand how swearing comes across to others and explain that in a work-related setting, where customers may be within earshot, swearing cannot be tolerated.

- Ask students to explain the meaning of swear words they use. Show them you are not phased/embarrassed by this.

- Keep a tally chart to show how many times they swear in a session. Set targets to improve their self control and reduce swearing. Issue rewards if they achieve a target.

- Take out a notepad and say 'I'm now recording what you are saying'.

- Use the paper with six boxes on it (as with lateness) for students to record when and what was said and why it was said.

- Give them an alternative word to use to express their frustration (for example, Old English words from 'Horrible Histories' like *mundungus* (smelly rubbish) or *curpin* (a chicken's bottom).

- Have a Swear Box – their name will go into it if they swear together with a note of the word used. At the end of the week sanction those with the most slips.

Refusing to work/defiance

- Check with them the reason for their refusal/non-co-operation. Do they understand the task?

- Avoid conflict – look at the student and address them by their name quietly, firmly, and with respect. Focus on the behaviour. Remind them about the rules and routines. Also remind them of their past successes. With a good relationship in place just letting them know you feel let down might be sufficient. Offer them the opportunity to retrieve the situation.

- Explain that their behaviour is not appropriate in terms of the Code of Behaviour. Preface this by telling them you think they can work well and that they need to make a decision about their behaviour. Give them time to reflect and then come back for their decision.

- Use humour to reduce emotional tension in some cases.

- Use the following script in difficult situations – 'If you choose to continue to [x] then I will have to [x], but if you choose another route then no sanction will be applied. I will give you two minutes to think it over'.

- Write names on the board of those students refusing to work (three strikes and they are out).

- In some cases it may be appropriate to ignore a behaviour and deal with it later.

- Sometimes you will need to calmly stand your ground, use the broken record technique, and repeat your instructions. Do this until the student engages in the work.

Shouting out in class

- In the establishment phase develop a clear policy on how questions will be answered. When students shout out remind them of the agreed policy.

- Ignore those who do shout out and reward and praise those students who do not shout out.

- If shouting out occurs, use a stopwatch and detain the student for the length of time your lesson was disturbed.

- Tactically ignoring some shouting out may be beneficial. Ignore the student until they conform.

- Reinforce the no shouting rule by reminding students of this prior to asking a question.

- Consider a 'no hands up' ethos whereby staff will nominate students to answer. You can put names on pieces of paper and draw these out from a container to randomly select students to answer.

Intimidatory behaviour

- Remain calm, cool and collected. Ensure your body language shows confidence.

- Do not always give students the desired and expected response.

- Do not be phased by criticism directed at you and instead reflect on it. Show your preparedness to accept/maybe change.

- Talk to other staff – is the same attitude shown towards them? If not – why not?

- Try befriending the student, who may then be less inclined to behave badly towards you.

- Get the support of a colleague or senior manager if you feel the situation is becoming serious.

- Allow a 'cool-off' period if necessary.

- Give the student a choice within the rules.

- Exercise zero tolerance with a clear exit strategy and follow-up:

    o issue a Red Card

    o use mentoring (for example, for anger management strategies)

    o involve the parents

    o instigate consequences

    o agree on a method of reparation.

Bad manners, including ignoring you and other anti-social behaviour such as flatulence

- When students are ignoring you:

    o try a humorous approach

    o take the route of minimum disruption – 'You are ignoring me now. I'll see you later'

    o plan an escape route – 'I have asked you twice. Are you going to do as I have asked or do we have to take it further?'

    o appeal to their sense of good manners (social acceptability).

- Anti-social behaviour (for example, flatulence):

    o ignore it, because by reacting you will give them exactly what they were trying to elicit

    o explain that if they do it again they will have to stay in at break for a lesson on healthy diets and the effect certain foods have on the digestion

- ○ show great concern for their health and tell them it might be a good idea if you were to talk to their parents about it immediately by telephone if they are having trouble controlling this

- ○ follow the normal procedure for disruptive behaviour but be careful not to appear confrontational or you will get the classic response, 'That's not fair, I can't help it'.

Eating/drinking in class

- Establish a mutually agreed no eating or drinking in class rule when you first meet the group (except for rehydration purposes in some settings):

  - ○ reinforce this with Health and Safety issues, particularly in practical areas

  - ○ in work areas there can also be issues of hygiene (for example, Hair and Beauty, Animal Care).

- If a student is found eating or drinking ask them to put the items away. If this is a soft drink do not allow them to finish it off. Remind them of what was initially agreed and offer to keep it safe for them.

- When students are eating move into their personal space bubble and say nothing. If they continue eating you can use a more humorous approach and say you'll join them in a moment with your sandwiches – but warn them that the filling is a particularly smelly fish. This is usually enough to put them off eating.

Drunkenness/effects of drugs

- The dangers of students arriving in college under the influence of drugs or alcohol are very clear. However detection is sometimes extremely difficult and can leave a lecturer vulnerable if an accusation is made.

- Colleges need to have clear policies relating to being on site under the influence of alcohol, drugs and other substances. The consequences for a violation of the rule need to be made clear.

- In induction programmes the policy needs to be discussed with learners. The implications on Health and Safety grounds and risk need to be outlined (for example, if there is reasonable suspicion then the student will be removed from the learning environment and asked to leave the site or be kept in a safe area until a carer can be contacted). Any action needs to be taken in light of the law and an appropriate referral may need to be made.

- Support needs to be given to high-risk students.

- In residential settings (for example, land-based colleges) clear rules need to be established about alcohol in dormitory areas and in common room/refectory areas on site.

Flirting in class/sexually related conversations

The disintegration of typical nuclear and extended families has meant that many students have not been taught appropriate boundaries. Together with the early sexualisation of young people through television, magazines and fashion this has meant that many students do not understand what constitutes acceptable and unacceptable behaviour:

- At the outset clear guidelines need to be established on acceptable behaviour and the acceptable content of conversations in the learning environment. Getting students to understand the reasons for this is important (for example, relating these to the world of work and what is acceptable in the workplace).

- When transgressions occur we need to give a firm response and challenge the conversation topic. Tell students what is not acceptable. If this is repeated make a record of what is said and say it will be passed to the tutor and contact will be made with home.

- If flirting amongst students is occurring (a natural behaviour) a lighter approach may be necessary – perhaps with a humorous manner and comment. Seat changes may also be necessary.

Reflection on practice

Using the table on the next page identify two types of challenging behaviour from among those discussed in this chapter and for each list the strategies you have used and indicate whether they were successful. Then list a further two new strategies you would use for each behaviour next term, based on those included in the chapter.

Key points

- The importance of developing a consistent approach:

  - consistency in language and response

  - consistency in models of emotional control

  - consistency in environment – behaviour management displays and consistent visual messages – and the importance of peripheral learning.

- It is important to develop a consistent approach in college to manage the variety of challenging behaviours you will meet:

  - Spend time with your team developing a Consistency Model where you will identify key behaviours and a variety of strategies that all of you will employ.

  - Identify the types of student behaviour that cause you the most concern and any strategies suggested in this chapter which would be suitable for use with these.

Reflection on practice: Strategies for facing challenging behaviour

Behaviour One:		
Your own strategies you have used when faced with this type of behaviour	Successful	Unsuccessful
New strategies you will try in the next term	Successful	Unsuccessful

Behaviour Two:		
Your own strategies you have used when faced with this type of behaviour	Successful	Unsuccessful
New strategies you will try in the next term	Successful	Unsuccessful

Photocopiable: *How to Manage Behaviour in Further Education* (Second Edition)
© David Vizard 2012

CHAPTER 9

Using the whole team

In the last chapter I emphasised the importance of all staff managing behaviour in a consistent manner. Good colleges will involve every member of staff in the management of behaviour and there will be a clear understanding amongst them on how they should respond to and deal with the range of behaviours they will meet. Each member must feel sufficiently empowered to manage a number of situations, and staff training in the effective management of behaviour is essential.

Support staff will come into contact with learners in both informal and formal settings.

Informal settings

Support staff will come into contact with students in informal settings away from the classroom. When some students come across site, security and catering staff in public areas they will not have the maturity to handle this interaction well: instead they will play to an audience and display 'showboating' behaviour. In such situations it is best to move students away to a setting where they will not be in the spotlight (a corner of the refectory perhaps, or if in a corridor, a short distance away from any audience) whilst also ensuring at all times that you do not make yourself vulnerable.

Some of the typical situations that might occur in a variety of informal settings are given below.

Reception/office/finance

- *Challenging parents/carers:* some parents and carers will often come into public areas and cause problems with their challenging and extreme behaviour. It is vital that you move them to another location and, if possible, get them seated in order to allow them to get whatever is bothering them off their chests. You will then need to reply to this. Asking the miracle question 'What would you like me to do to remedy this situation?' can take the wind out of their sails. Staff teams can also develop specific roles to play when dealing with a variety of situations:

○ 'The Rottweiler': takes no prisoners and can be very firm.

○ 'The Carer': listens, provides tissues and a shoulder to cry on.

○ 'The Problem Solver': tries to find a solution whilst showing empathy.

Managing telephone calls from aggressive and angry parents can be challenging. However, allowing them to let off steam before responding can often prove beneficial. Buying time and saying you will need to investigate, as well as giving them a time-span within which you will respond, can be helpful as well. Support staff will often report that parents can be ruder than their children. Remember that if a call becomes threatening and extremely abusive it is essential that you terminate it, afterwards reporting the matter to your line manager.

- *Challenging/upset students:* students can express a range of concerns when they see you: that things are not right on a course, that they have timetable problems, that they are concerned about exam results or problems with their EMA (Education Maintenance Allowance) or LSF (Learner Support Fund), and so on. The strategies you need to use are similar to those with challenging parents. Listen to the problem, allow the student to unload their feelings, and then try to find a solution.

Case Study A

Office staff in one college find managing the behaviour of students congregating outside their office a particular challenge. How would you manage the following situations they identified as problems?

- Students stage phoning (talking loudly on mobiles) and discussing inappropriate topics relating to the drugs they took at the weekend.

  _____
  _____
  _____
  _____

- Male students engaging in 'play fighting' outside the office which causes them to fall into the office space.

  _____
  _____
  _____
  _____

- Students swearing loudly at one another along the length of the corridor.

  _____
  _____
  _____
  _____

(Continued)

(Continued)

- A male and female student passionately kissing one another in the entrance hall outside the office.

_____

_____

_____

_____

Case Study B

The behaviour of some teaching staff can be extreme when, for example, you ask them to attend training or implement a new policy. How would you manage a situation where a lecturer storms into your office, leans over your desk threateningly, and shouts at you about an e-mail you have just sent out relating to a new procedure set up by the college management team?

_____

_____

_____

_____

_____

Site staff, including the security team

Often students will deliberately challenge staff in uniform, such as security staff. As part of their way of life they will have learnt to challenge authority figures. Many will have met security staff in shopping centres/nightclubs and will displace their resentment from these settings onto college security staff.

Security staff will normally work in teams of three or four. It is important that team members understand their roles clearly. One team I worked with ascribed certain roles to its members. One had a listening role, to let students describe their feelings on a situation: another had a 'tough, no messing role', and presented a very firm figure. Another team I worked with were very pro-active, seeing a real problem with 14- to 16-year-old learners who had two hours' worth of unsupervised time in the middle of the day because of timetabling problems. This had led to lots of damage, graffiti on site, and students wandering along the corridors disturbing other groups, so they had decided to set up a five-a-side football activity during this time in the sports hall. This intervention had reduced the problem behaviour and was also a way of developing positive relationships between the security team and students.

Often the security team will have to deal with adults trying to gain entry to the site: they will also encounter students who have forgotten their passes and on occasions some will need to be removed from the learning environment. The skills that security staff have for diffusing conflict and confrontation can be utilised to train other staff.

Site staff will also often have to deal with students damaging property, smoking on site, and dropping litter and cigarette ends. Students can be very adept at challenging staff in these situations and taking their poor behaviour to the limit. They will also test staff by attempting to get them to lose their temper. A form of entrapment can take place. It is important that staff are aware of this and have strategies in place both to keep calm and remain in control (see Chapter 6).

Refectory/catering staff

Students will use these areas at a variety of times throughout the day, making their supervision extremely difficult. Also the additives and ingredients in some products can cause poor behaviour within a short time of their consumption, which then exacerbates the situation. Some stealing of food and damage to vending machines might occur. In addition students can be abusive to staff.

It is important that there is a clear policy for managing behaviour in these areas and that there is a clear support structure available, such as the ability to call security or other support staff. Identifying students using photo files may also be of value.

Formal settings

Learning resource/library staff

Library staff contribute directly to the learning process, teaching research skills to students and developing their other skills to ensure that they are able to study independently. One main challenge to working in library areas is that students of differing ages and from a variety of groups will have come to study without lecturer supervision. Most resources/library areas are zones where quiet working is expected. However some students will find this a real challenge. In one library they have helped to overcome this by giving students key study/research skills which will enable them to study independently. They have also zoned the library into red, amber and green zones. The red zone is a silence zone so learners can study and work without disturbances. The amber zone is one where quiet talking is allowed and the green zone is one where learners can move around freely, be active in their learning and discuss their work openly with other learners. This system has been shown to work very well.

With many libraries now reducing their book stock and up to 90 per cent of materials being electronic, this has introduced the need for a new range of skills for learners and support staff. Widespread use of the internet has also provoked another challenge, with students attempting to access inappropriate sites. It is possible to block most of these, but some students will be able to circumvent these systems. Software is available to monitor live usage and some colleges have introduced staff team members who will monitor this and move in quickly to challenge those students who may be on inappropriate sites – together with evidence that could be sent to their parents/carers.

Learning support workers/mentors/counsellors/guidance

Work by these staff could be compromised by them adopting an overly disciplinarian approach. Much of their work is based on trust. In fact, these staff members need to have the following qualities:

- Good listening skills.

- Able to display positive non-verbal communication.

- Able to encourage.

- Aim to raise self-esteem.

- Able to act as a role model.

- Can show empathy.

- Open and able to share their life experiences.

- Supportive.

- Non-judgemental.

Thus when dealing with learners it is vital that they use strategies that will not compromise their role.

Key behaviour management strategies for support staff

- When dealing with challenging behaviour do not conduct interactions in a public forum – remove students from the oxygen of publicity.

- Keep your focus on the behaviour, do not personalise it.

- Remember that positioning is important:

  ○ move learners to a new position (much like a football referee when they are about to issue a yellow card to a player)

  ○ do not have your back to a number of learners – position yourself with the wall behind you

  ○ always have an escape route

  ○ stand at right angles to a learner as this will avoid excessive eye contact.

- Do not invade a student's personal space bubble (46 cm around most people). An angry student will have a larger space bubble.

- Do not get dragged into arguments. The student will try to display a range of secondary behaviours to divert your attention from the primary behaviour you are addressing. Examples include huffing, looking away and tutting. Re-focus the learner by repeating the primary behaviour/misdemeanour you are addressing.

- Focus on the required behaviour – say what the student should be doing, not what they shouldn't be doing.

- Avoid over-verbalising.

- Speak slowly, vary your pace, and lower your pitch.

- Use silence and pauses. Leaving three to five seconds after a statement, together with eye contact, can be a powerful tool.

- Use open body language and maintain a relaxed position.

- Stay positive.

- Use attention diverters.

- Allow the student and yourself time out or time to reflect.

- Keep your own respect and theirs intact.

- Allow the student to save face by giving them an escape route.

- Use de-escalation skills.

- Do not be manically vigilant – tactically ignore some things.

Reflection on practice

Below are six real scenarios presented by support staff in which they have faced challenging behaviour.

Read each one and select which of the strategies given would be best to use. Then add another appropriate strategy of your own.

Scenario 1: Learning resource centre

A student is asked by the librarian to leave the library after several warnings. He has made rude noises, played music on his MP3 player, and played games on the computer. He refuses to leave and then threatens to 'knock the librarian's block off'.

Strategy 1: Call for the security team to remove the student. This threat is serious and likely to lead to a severe consequence for the learner, so you must ensure the incident is recorded and its details are passed on to your line manager.

Strategy 2: Call for colleague support and request that the student leaves.

Personal strategy:

Scenario 2: ICT suite

A support tutor is frequently being asked to help a student in a busy ICT session. The student's demands are unrealistic and she is wanting personal attention. She becomes frustrated and finally becomes very abusive with the support tutor, who is trying to support learners with Special Educational Needs.

(Continued)

(Continued)

Strategy 1: The support tutor would need to outline the problem to the lecturer working with the group and get their support and help with the student.

Strategy 2: Explain to the student that you are busy with another student but that you will help them when you have finished.

Strategy 3: Elicit the support of another student to help until further support becomes available.

Personal strategy:

Scenario 3: Site staff

Three students from the Creative and Media area are dumping bags of rubbish at the back of the block in front of fire doors. When the caretaker asks them to remove it and place it in the correct area they ignore him and walk off muttering.

Strategy 1: Follow the students back to their classroom, speak to the lecturer about what has just happened, and ensure they rectify the situation and apologise.

Strategy 2: Follow the students and speak to them about the Health and Safety issues of what they have done and the likely consequence of blocking fire doors.

Strategy 3: Ignore the incident and clear away the rubbish, as it will take less time.

Personal strategy:

Scenario 4: Refectory/catering

A group of students are rude to staff serving hot food at the servery; they say that the food portions are too small and that they are not going to pay for these and they then swear at the staff.

Strategy 1: Tell the students that refusing to pay is their choice, and retain the food.

Strategy 2: Tell the students that there are consultative procedures that they can use (for example, the College Consultative Committee, or Student Union representatives). They should use these to air their views.

Strategy 3: Clearly remind students about college policy relating to swearing and remind them of the consequences if they continue. Use of a photo file may be needed to identify the relevant students.

Personal strategy:

Scenario 5: Learning support assistant

A learning support worker is attempting to help a student with Special Educational Needs who is refusing the help and support being offered. Other students in the room are teasing the student because he is receiving help.

Strategy 1: Discuss the actions of other students with the lecturer and explain how this is restricting the help you can give to the student with SEN. Ask the lecturer to talk to the students concerned.

Strategy 2: Discuss with the student you are supporting the reasons for their refusal to accept help and offer alternative strategies.

Strategy 3: Discuss with the student whether working with them in an alternative location might be better.

Personal strategy:

Scenario 6: Exam/assessment co-ordination

An assessment is underway when the exam co-ordinator is called to the room because a group of vocational students are talking loudly and disturbing other students. They will not do anything the invigilator is asking them to do. As exam co-ordinator would you:

Strategy 1: Quickly get the relevant details from the invigilator and give quiet instructions to students who have been talking loudly. State that they can continue with the assessment if they agree to conform to the silence rule. Tell them that their scripts will have to have a note attached detailing the incident at the end. Observe them to ensure compliance.

Strategy 2: If the exam board's regulations have been broken, remove them from the room and get them to finish the assessment in another area. Talk to the subject co-ordinator about the incident, contact the exam board, and if appropriate their parents.

Personal strategy:

Support staff will have a range of skills in the management of behaviour that they could share with and develop with lecturers as well. I believe that they are a powerful, under-used resource and that colleges should utilise them fully by developing a team approach to managing behaviour. This will help to develop a consistent approach to behaviour management amongst *all* staff.

Key points

- The induction programme for support staff must include behaviour management strategies.

- Adopting a teamwork approach between lecturers and support staff is beneficial in relation to behaviour management.

- Support staff need to feel empowered to manage challenging behaviour and therefore require appropriate strategies in order to do this.

- Understanding key strategies to use with learners in typical settings is vital. These strategies will vary depending on individual roles and whether these take place in a formal or informal setting.

CHAPTER 10

Staff development activities

The 20 activities contained in this chapter are regularly used on staff development/training days by the author. These are photocopiable resources which can be freely utilised within the purchaser's institution for staff development purposes.

- The instructions are written from the facilitator's viewpoint.

- Group sizes for the activities will vary:

  - Activity 1 – a minimum of at least 15 delegates will be needed.

  - Activities 5 and 14 – at least nine delegates will be required.

  - All other activities will work with numbers that can split into multiples of two, three or five people.

ACTIVITY 1: OUR TOP TEN

Area: To identify key types of poor behaviour

Resources: Flipchart paper per group

Group Size: Five people in each

Duration: 20 minutes

- Ask each group of five people to decide on their own Top Ten of Challenging Behaviours, with Number 1 being the most intrusive and challenging behaviour.

- Ask three groups of five to join together and refine their three lists into one Top Ten.

- Ask one member from each group of 15 to take their Top Ten and meet with the leaders of other groups.

- A super Top Ten can then be produced.

- This list can be used as a basis for other activities during the day – for example, the Consistency Model Activity (see Chapter 8).

 Photocopiable: *How to Manage Behaviour in Further Education* **(Second Edition)**
© David Vizard 2012

ACTIVITY 2: AUDITS FOR STAFF

Area: Development of audits for staff to use to make their learning environments conducive to good work and behaviour

Resources: Worksheet for the task given below. One of these is used per group. (Also see Reflection on practice: Classroom Audit Sheets in Chapter 3)

Group Size: Three people in each

Duration: 20 minutes

- Ask delegates to 'thought shower' the key areas involved in ensuring that learning environments are conducive for good work and behaviour. Examples could include:

  - Different learning styles.

  - Rules and routines.

  - Consistency in behaviour management.

  - Positive behaviour management.

  - Use of support staff.

  - Peripheral learning.

  - Differentiation.

  - Assessment for learning.

  - Relationships.

  - Furniture arrangement and seating plans.

- From this list select five areas and ask group members to make up 20 questions/ statements for each area for the task sheet.

- *Questions 1–10* will require Yes or No responses. The questions must be phrased so that the Yes response is the one that would lead to a conducive environment for good work and behaviour.

- For *Questions 11–20* list 10 statements and ask that staff develop a 1–5 scoring system for each statement, with 5 being when there is a strong agreement with the statement and 1 when there is a strong disagreement with the statement. Once again the statements will outline a desired position to do with good work and behaviour.

- Ask them to join together with two other groups and compare their questions/statements.

Photocopiable: *How to Manage Behaviour in Further Education* (Second Edition)
© David Vizard 2012

Classroom audit

Circle YES or NO for these statements:

1   YES/NO

2   YES/NO

3   YES/NO

4   YES/NO

5   YES/NO

6   YES/NO

7   YES/NO

8   YES/NO

9   YES/NO

10 YES/NO

TOTAL NUMBER OF 'YES' RESPONSES TO STATEMENTS 1–10   ……

Circle 1, 2, 3, 4 or 5 where 1 = STRONGLY DISAGREE and 5 = STRONGLY AGREE:

11 1 2 3 4 5

12 1 2 3 4 5

13 1 2 3 4 5

14 1 2 3 4 5

15 1 2 3 4 5

16 1 2 3 4 5

17 1 2 3 4 5

18 1 2 3 4 5

19 1 2 3 4 5

20 1 2 3 4 5

TOTAL SCORE FOR RESPONSES TO STATEMENTS 11–20   ……

ACTIVITY 3: A POSITIVE LEARNING ENVIRONMENT – 10 Rs

Area: Developing a positive learning environment

Resources: Worksheet for the task given below. Provide one per group

Group Size: Two people in each

Duration: 20 minutes

The 10 Rs of positive behaviour management were given in Chapter 3.

- In groups of two, ask staff to list how they would utilise these 10 areas in their learning environments. For example, how would they establish the rules and routines initially and maintain these throughout the year? Ask them to jot down any of the ways by which they would develop these areas on the sheet provided.

The 10 Rs of positive behaviour management

Rules	
Routines	
Recognition	
Rapport	
Respect	
Relationships	
Rights	
Responsibility	
Resilience	
Rewards	

Photocopiable: *How to Manage Behaviour in Further Education* **(Second Edition)**
© David Vizard 2012

ACTIVITY 4: A POSITIVE MARKETPLACE

Area: Identifying how we develop positive learning environments

Resources: None

Group Size: Whole group – a marketplace activity

Duration: 10 minutes

- Tell the group that this will be a marketplace activity where they will stand and move around the room to meet three other lecturers. When meeting each colleague they must share good practice by discussing how they create positive learning environments:

  - Verbally – the key positive phrases they use.

  - Non-verbally – the gestures they use towards students to show approval.

  - Through the use of tangibles/rewards – describing the reward systems they use.

Photocopiable: *How to Manage Behaviour in Further Education* **(Second Edition)**
© David Vizard 2012

ACTIVITY 5: SEE AND HEAR

Area: Reflecting on learning environments where there is good or inappropriate behaviour

Resources: Flipchart paper per group

Group Size: Three people in each

Duration: 20 minutes

- Ask the staff to divide into groups of three.

- Ask each group to consider for five minutes what they might see and hear in a learning environment where there is inappropriate behaviour.

- Then ask the group to consider for five minutes what they might see and hear in a learning environment where there is good behaviour.

- Request that each group joins with two other groups to agree on a list of key factors for positive learning environments.

Photocopiable: *How to Manage Behaviour in Further Education* **(Second Edition)**
© David Vizard 2012

ACTIVITY 6: BLOCKING AND THE 'BROKEN RECORD' TECHNIQUE

Area: Assertiveness and conflict management

Resources: Paper for all participants

Group Size: Three people in each

Duration: 15 minutes

In order to manage some forms of poor behaviour and counter arguments from students it may be necessary to block their responses and utilise the 'broken record' technique. Adopting these techniques can also be beneficial when we are being assertive.

'Blocking' involves ignoring the comment made by a student and repeating our re-directing statement – rather like the repetition of the same line in a song when a crack in a record causes the needle to stick and repeat the same line.

- Ask staff to divide into groups of three with one person being the student, another the lecturer, and the third person being an observer.

- Ask each group to re-enact one of these situations which may cause a dispute:

    ○ a student arriving 10 minutes late to a lesson for the third time this week

    ○ a student failing to hand in a piece of coursework following a third extension.

- Ask the group members to swap roles and attempt another re-enactment.

- Get all staff back together to analyse the best scripts to use when using the blocking and broken record technique.

ACTIVITY 7: ROLE PLAY

Area: Developing positive body language

Resources: Worksheet for the task below per group

Group Size: Three people in each

Duration: 20 minutes

- Ask staff to divide into groups of three.

- Ask each group member to chose a role – student, lecturer or observer.

- Ask them to establish a scenario they would like to enact. This should be one where there is a disagreement between the lecturer and student.

- For five minutes get them to carry out the role play – with the observer recording on the sheet the body language of the lecturer and student in two different ways: body language that helped to resolve the disagreement and body language that was less than helpful.

- After doing so ask them to swap roles.

- Finally, ask them what are their conclusions from the activity in relation to the importance of body language?

Developing positive body language

Scenario

	Helpful body language	Unhelpful body language
Student		
Lecturer		

Photocopiable: *How to Manage Behaviour in Further Education* **(Second Edition)**
© David Vizard 2012

ACTIVITY 8: POSITIVELY DISAGREE

Area: Developing rapport with learners

Resources: None

Group Size: Two people in each

Duration: 10 minutes

- Ask the staff to form into groups of two and select a topic about which they hold differing views.

- Get them to discuss this topic and as they do so to disagree with each other. They should also use rapport building strategies the whole time (as given in Chapter 5) – matching; mirroring body language; using the language of sensory preference; adopting similar styles of speech.

- At the end of five minutes ask each pair to reflect on what happened towards the end of the discussion after the rapport building strategies were used.

ACTIVITY 9: TRUE LIES!

Area: Developing positive body language

Resources: Worksheet for the task below for each participant

Group Size: Three people in each

Duration: 15 minutes

- Ask the staff to form groups of three. Then ask them to take turns listing four facts about themselves – three that are true and one that is a lie.

- The other two in the group must record on their sheets the body language of the member who is completing the task.

- As a group they should try to identify which of each of the facts were lies.

- They should also list the body language that indicated to them it was a lie.

- They should assess how successful they were as a group by starting with a maximum of 12 marks, and for each person's incorrect guess deduct one mark up to a maximum of four.

True Lies!

Four facts about yourself:

1

2

3

4

Second person in group:

Body language

1

2

3

4

Third person in group:

Body language

1

2

3

4

Your Group's Score _____

ACTIVITY 10: THE FOUR Fs OF CONFRONTATION

Area: Confrontation

Resources: Flipchart paper – five sheets per group

Group Size: Five people in each

Duration: 20 minutes

When faced with confrontation students will often be taken over by the emotion they are experiencing. All rational thought becomes impossible. We have a strong emotional arousal and we may respond in a less than appropriate manner. One of four F responses may occur:

- Fight

- Flight

- Freeze

- Flock.

- Ask staff to get into groups of five and use a sheet of flipchart paper for each of these F responses. They must list the types of situations which may cause students to respond in this manner.

- In the end they will have four sheets with a list of situations where students will respond with an F response.

- Ask the groups to list on the fifth sheet some strategies that they could use when faced with these types of responses.

- Display each group's work and in a plenary session identify the best strategies.

Photocopiable: *How to Manage Behaviour in Further Education* **(Second Edition)**
© David Vizard 2012

ACTIVITY 11: ACTIVE LISTENING

Area: Conflict management, positive behaviour management

Resources: Flipchart paper per group

Group Size: Three people in each

Duration: 15 minutes

For effective communication the listener should always try to engage with the speaker by listening actively.

- Divide staff into groups of three and ask them to make a list of the five key characteristics of an active listener:

    ○ They must face the speaker and look into their eyes.

    ○ They must be relaxed and not interrupt or fidget.

    ○ They should summarise the speaker's key points.

    ○ If they do not understand something, at a suitable break they should ask for clarification.

    ○ They should nod in agreement.

- Once these characteristics have been identified, two members of the group should then start a conversation on music or food and utilise their active listening skills. The third member of the group should observe.

- The observer should then feed back their views.

- The two involved in the conversation should think about the following:

    ○ What was the easiest and most difficult thing about being an active listener?

    ○ Why is it important to be a good listener?

ACTIVITY 12: THE LANGUAGE OF CHOICE

Area: Scripts we use with students

Resources: Paper for each group

Group Size: Two people in each

Duration: 10 minutes

Our choice of words and how we say them are key to the successful management of behaviour. It is always wise to prepare scripts to use in different situations. Remember that the less we say the better. Also assume a pleasant tone as calm words are likely to result in calm students. Avoid overly apologetic or pleading language.

Some of the scripts we can adopt are as follows:

- 'If you choose to break the rules then you must understand the consequences you are bringing on yourself'.

- 'What is the rule for answering questions? Then please use it. Thank you'.

Some students will try to divert your attention by using some secondary behaviour, perhaps by producing a counter-argument: 'You're always picking on me'. It is important that we keep our focus, block their response, and repeat our instruction.

We can also give students a choice and some 'cooling off' time to reflect on the situation: 'You realise that if you keep chewing gum the consequence you will bring on yourself is that you will lose your breaktime. However, if you put the gum in the bin you will keep your break. I am going to give you a few minutes to think about it'.

- Discuss the points made above and then split staff into groups of two.

- Ask each group to think of a situation where they might be able to use their Language of Choice.

- With one person acting as the student and the other as a lecturer practise using the script.

- Then reverse roles.

Photocopiable: *How to Manage Behaviour in Further Education* **(Second Edition)**
© David Vizard 2012

ACTIVITY 13: HOW YOUR COLLEGE CAN HELP STUDENTS DEVELOP THEIR OWN STRATEGIES TO MANAGE BEHAVIOUR

Area: Scripts we use with students

Resources: A worksheet for the task below per group

Group Size: Five people in each

Duration: 15 minutes

Many young learners find it extremely difficult to manage their emotions and feelings. We often tell students not to behave in a particular way without giving them the requisite skills and strategies necessary to avoid that same behaviour and to manage their feelings and emotions.

- Split staff into groups of five and ask each group to reflect on what they are doing currently in the areas on the worksheet and what they could do to develop these areas in the future.

How we are helping students develop their own strategies

	What we are currently doing	What we could do in the future
Raising learner self-esteem		
Using dramatherapy/role play with learners to manage anger		
Helping students to understand the influence of body language and position		
Developing active listening skills and reducing communication blockers		
Developing a script containing positive statements/affirmations for students when facing a difficult situation		
Developing an alternative view/mindset – for example, someone bumping into you may not have done so intentionally		
Using/developing relaxation strategies with students – for example, breathing, counting and visualisation		
Using mediators		
Understanding the cycles of anger: • Signs/triggers • Actions to avoid		
Use of mirroring behaviour and modelling approaches to help students reflect on their own responses		

Photocopiable: *How to Manage Behaviour in Further Education* **(Second Edition)**
© David Vizard 2012

ACTIVITY 14: WHEELS WITHIN WHEELS

Area: Dealing with inappropriately behaving groups

Resources: Paper for recorders in each group

Group Size: Nine people in each, subdivided into threes

Duration: 25 minutes

- Each group is made up of nine people and this is then subdivided into three groups of three. Each group of three is given a different scenario.

- Below are three behavioural issues that are typical when working with challenging groups:

  1. In a group of 25 students there are two main groups of students affiliated to different youth communities or gangs. Most sessions involve very negative comments being passed between the two groups. A number of threats are regularly made. How could we best manage this situation? (See Chapter 7.)

  2. A group of older students (aged 19 and above) are having to follow a course to enable them to qualify to receive benefits. If they fail to attend their benefits will be cut. They do not wish to be there and are causing much disruption. Meanwhile other students in the group want to get on with their work. What sort of intervention would you use?

  3. A mixed group of 25 students will not engage in work and are spending most of the time flirting with the opposite sex in the room. They are also spending a lot of the time using their mobile phones to send inappropriate messages and pictures to one another. What would be an appropriate intervention here?

- Each group of three must spend five minutes on their behaviour. One group member needs to record the findings and they then move to the next group (in a clockwise direction), taking their behaviour with them. This group then spends five minutes adding strategies to the list. All group recorders must move at the same time to the new groups, taking their behaviour with them. There will be three moves in all, with the group recorder returning to their original group where they will share the strategies from the other two groups for their initial behaviour.

- Each group then feeds back the various strategies to all the other staff delegates.

ACTIVITY 15: SNOWBALLING

Area: Improving consistency

Resources: A copy of 15 behaviours and the strategies to use with each (given in Chapter 8)

Group Size: Five people in each

Duration: 20 minutes

- In Chapter 8 we looked at 15 behaviours and strategies were given to manage these.

- In groups of five ask staff to look through the strategies given.

- Ask them if they can add any extra strategies for these behaviours.

- Ask them to add in any extra behaviours they think have been omitted.

- Now ask each group to join with another group of five and share the additional strategies they have developed.

- Finally, ask the groups to examine all the additional behaviours they have come up with and discuss the possible strategies they could use with these.

ACTIVITY 16: IDENTIFYING KEY STUDENT ROLES IN BADLY BEHAVING GROUPS

Area: Dealing with badly behaving groups

Resources: Sheet with the list of student roles per group

Group Size: Five people in each

Duration: 10 minutes

Students will play different roles in each class. The key to successful behaviour management is to identify these roles and use this knowledge to your advantage. Gaining the upper hand with alpha males and alpha females in the group is vital for successful behaviour management.

- Split staff into groups of five and ask each group to identify a class of students who will offer high levels of challenging behaviour.

- Using the list, ask staff to ascribe the roles that key members of the class play and identify some strategies that may help to develop a good working atmosphere.

- Discuss what kind of whole-class reward systems could be developed to promote good relationships.

Some students' key roles

- *Alpha male:* Above-average intelligence, usually physically bigger.

- *Alpha female*: Above-average intelligence, dressed in the latest fashions, uses sarcasm to control those around her.

- *Instigator:* Starts trouble but usually gets away with this by being surreptitious.

- *Regulator/Questioner:* Constantly interrupts by asking the same question in many different ways.

- *Deflector:* Takes the heat off the student in trouble by deflecting your attention using smart comments or minor misbehaviour.

- *Orchestrator:* The student who co-ordinates much of the bad behaviour by acting as a 'conductor' for the 'symphony' of bad behaviour.

- *Class Clown:* The class entertainer, who can be difficult to manage.

- *Fall Guy:* Male or female student who is happy to take the rap for things.

- *Challenger:* Enjoys challenging the rules and instructions given to them. They will often 'grandstand' by making a late entrance in order to gain plaudits from their peer group.

ACTIVITY 17: CROSS CULTURAL COMMUNICATION

Area: Cross cultural communication

Resources: None

Group Size: Two people in each

Duration: 20 minutes

In Chapter 5 we looked at the cultural dimension in relation to body language.

This exercise will reflect upon cross cultural communication which refers to interpersonal communication and interaction with students from different cultures. It is concerned with overcoming cultural differences across nationalities, traditions, religions, cultures and behaviours.

The diversity of students in our educational institution means an element of cross cultural communication will always be needed. An awareness of cultural differences can favourably impact on the success of our classroom management and behaviour control.

Students from the South Asian region, from the Indian Sub-Continent, including India, Pakistan and Bangladesh

There is a clear communication hierarchy which is the basis for social organisation. Young people are expected to perform well in education and to create a role model within the family for others to follow. Parents will be very influential in a young person's choice of educational pathway. There are now second and third generations, some of whom will find it highly difficult to relate to their culture. Some will create their own subculture or adapt to other cultures. This can lead to some young people being outlawed and having to lead an independent life outside of their families. Because of this they can be confused and disturbed which can then affect their performance in college.

Growing up in two distinctive cultural traditions and value systems which conflict over issues such as the role of women in society and adherence to religious and cultural traditions can cause problems. The conflicting demands made by home and college on behaviour, loyalties and obligations can also be a source of psychological conflict and tension in Asian youngsters.

- In pairs ask staff to discuss the following, recording any key points. Then ask them to join with another group and compare their responses.

  1 How does their college deliver cross cultural awareness training?

  2 Given the value of honouring the family which is deeply ingrained in South Asian families and that discussing any personal problems with an outsider is regarded as a disgrace to the family, how does their college provide culture-sensitive counselling?

  3 What types of challenging behaviours do they face from students from South Asian families? Note the strategies that work best?

  4 How does their college work with parents/guardians when dealing with complex situations with this group?

Photocopiable: *How to Manage Behaviour in Further Education* **(Second Edition)**
© David Vizard 2012

ACTIVITY 18: AN ASSERTIVENESSS 'THOUGHT SHOWER'

Area: Assertiveness

Resources: Flipchart paper per group

Group Size: Five people in each

Duration: 20 minutes

- Divide staff into groups of five.

- Ask each group to 'thought shower' all the words that come into their heads to do with assertiveness onto the flipchart paper for five minutes.

- Then ask each group to subdivide the list into positive and negative words by placing a plus sign next to positive words and a minus sign next to negative words.

- Ask each group member to discuss any words that link with their approach when they are being assertive.

- Finally, request that each group produces their own definition of assertiveness.

- These, together with lists of words, should then be displayed.

- At this point the facilitator might also like to display their own definition of assertiveness.

Photocopiable: *How to Manage Behaviour in Further Education* **(Second Edition)**
© David Vizard 2012

ACTIVITY 19: BEING ASSERTIVE WITH STUDENTS

Area: Assertiveness

Resources: List of assertiveness strategies per group

Group Size: Three in each

Duration: 15 minutes

- Divide staff into groups of three. One group member is to take the role of lecturer, another of student, and the third of observer.

- Select a scenario where a lecturer is having to reprimand a student. The student should be argumentative.

- The lecturer must practise assertiveness techniques in dealing with the obstructive and argumentative student. Some strategies/approaches that could be used are listed below.

- Ask the observer to feed back their comments:

  ○ How successful was the assertive approach?

  ○ Are there any other assertiveness techniques that could have been used?

- Change the roles and repeat.

Assertiveness strategies/approaches

- Decide what you want.

- Ask for it clearly.

- Be calm and relaxed.

- Give and take criticism.

- Have a confident tone in your speech and fluctuate the levels. Use silence.

- State how you would like a behaviour to improve.

- Think carefully about your non-verbal behaviour – for example, avoid nervous movements.

- Try to end the conversation positively.

ACTIVITIES 20: WHAT DO YOU DO NEXT?

Area: Case studies for lecturers

Resources: Case Studies A–J below ⁻

Group Size: Three people in each

Duration: 15 minutes

Ask the staff to divide into groups of three.

Give each group a scenario to deal with (from Case Studies A–J). Ask the groups to list the strategies they would use.

Ask two groups of three to join together to describe their strategies and encourage each group to offer further strategies to the other.

Case Studies

Case Study A

An adult group of learners (35 years of age and older) are being confrontational, rude and aggressive, and are questioning the authority of a younger lecturer. Many have an arrogant attitude and will try to catch the lecturer out by asking difficult questions. Some students in the group are not engaging in this behaviour and are becoming frustrated as a result because it is impacting on their learning.

Case Study B

In a lesson a student repeatedly displays low-level challenges. The student is attention seeking, disruptive, and frequently off-task.

Case Study C

A group of students in class are unco-operative and are working together to provide a destructive influence.

Case Study D

A student arrives five minutes late to a lesson for the second time in a week. They do not have a reason for their lateness and display a 'so what' attitude.

Case Study E

A male student arrives at a Motor Vehicle workshop smelling strongly of alcohol. He is swaying slightly and finding it hard to focus his eyes.

Case Study F

A group of 20 girls (aged 16 to 18) in a Business Administration group frequently arrive late and continually use their mobile phones, engage in social chatting, and display off-task behaviours. There is also often a sexual tension in the room between students and a lot of swearing occurs. Very little work is completed in any session.

Case Study G

A Supporting Learning tutor notices that a number of students in the room will go on Facebook when they are asked to do anything online.

Case Study H

A male student comes into the classroom wearing the headphones belonging to his MP3 player. The music is playing loudly and he cannot hear anything you say. You ask him to remove the headphones and he fails to hear you. He then looks down, refusing to make any eye contact with you.

Case Study I

A student is using her mobile phone discretely under the desk to send a text message to another student in the room. The other student, on receiving the message, becomes extremely distressed.

Case Study J

A 16-year-old student enters the room in a loud manner after you have started the lesson. She sits down and starts swearing at other students. She then nudges and annoys the students sitting next to her. Later on she makes the worksheets into paper aeroplanes and throws these across the room.

Photocopiable: *How to Manage Behaviour in Further Education* (Second Edition)
© David Vizard 2012

Berry, I. (2003) *ALITE Newsletter* (November). Available at www.alite.co.uk/newsletters/2003/november. htm (accessed 12 October 2006).

Besag, V. (2006*) Understanding Girls' Friendships, Fights and Feuds: A Practical Approach to Girls' Bullying.* Maidenhead: Open University Press.

Blakemore, S. and Frith, U. (2005) *The Learning Brain: Lessons for Education.* Oxford: Blackwell.

Borg, J. (2008) *Body Language.* Harlow: Pearson Education.

Chandler, J. (2006) *Oppositional Defiant Disorder (ODD) and Conduct Disorder (CD) in Children and Adolescents: Diagnosis and Treatment.* Available at www.klis.com/chandler/pamphlet/oddcd/ oddcdpamphlet.htm (accessed 13 April 2006).

Churches, R. and Terry, R. (2007) *NLP for Teachers.* Carmarthen: Crown House.

Collett, P. (2004) *The Book of Tells.* London: Bantam.

DCSF (2009) G*angs and Group Offending: Guidance for Schools.* London: HMSO.

DCSF / Home Office (2010) S*afeguarding Children and Young People who may be Affected by Gang Activity.* London: HMSO.

DfE (2010a) Green Paper on Special Education Needs and Disabilities (March), Sarah Teather, Children's Minister. London: HMSO.

DfE (2010b) *Children with Special Education Needs 2010: An Analysis.* Available at https://www. education.gov.uk/publications/standard/publicationDetail/Page1/DFE-00553-2010 (accessed 30 November 2011).

DfES (2006) *Safeguarding Children and Safer Recruitment in Education.* Notts: DfES.

Diprose, J. and Burge, N. (2003) *Syndromes and Disorders.* South Devon: Care Consultancy.

Eccles, L. (2010) 'Angry young girls', *Daily Mail,* 29 November.

Elliott, M. (2005) *Bullying Pocketbook.* Arlesford: Teachers Pocketbooks.

Elliott, M. and Kilpatrick, J. (1994) *How to Stop Bullying: A KidscapeTraining Guide.* London: Kidscape.

Feinstein, J. and Kuumba, N.I. (2006) *A Toolkit for Resolving Group Conflict.* London: Jessica Kingsley.

Fisher, M. (2005) *Beating Anger.* London: Random House/Rider.

Food Standards Agency (2006) *Drinking Enough?* Available at www.eatwell.gov.uk/healthydiet/ nutritionessentials/drinks/drinkingenough (accessed 14 December 2006).

Frieman, B. (2001) *What Teachers Need to Know About Children at Risk.* New York: McGraw-Hill.

Gardner, H. and Hatch, T. (1989) 'Multiple intelligences go to school: educational implications of the theory of multiple intelligences', *Educational Researcher, 18* (8): 4–9.

George, B. (1995) *Gifted Education: Identification and Process.* London: David Fulton.

Ginott, H. (1972) *Teacher and Child.* New York: Macmillan.

Greenfield, S. (2007) *Times Educational Supplement Magazine* (12 January). Source NHS Info Centre (2006).

Hall, E.T. (1959) *The Silent Language.* New York: Doubleday.

Home Office (2011) *Gangs, You and Your Child.* Available at www.direct.gov.uk/gangs

Jackson, C. (2004) *Ladette Culture on the Increase in the Classroom.* Available at http://news.lancs.ac.uk/ Web/News/Pages/D9A0525F9BC3430B80256F1000448601.aspx (accessed 22 July 2011).

Jackson, C. (2006) *'Lads' and 'Ladettes' in School: Gender and a Fear of Failure.* Maidenhead: Open University Press.

James, J. (2008) *The Body Language Bible.* Reading: Ebury.

Jensen, E. (2005) 'Highly effective strategies for managing AD/HD', *Brain Store Teaching Tip of the Month* (Newsletter – April). Available at www.thebrainstore.com (accessed 7 May 2005).

Kuhne, M., Schachar, R. and Tannock, R. (1997) 'Impact of comorbid oppositional or conduct problems on Attention-Deficit Hyperactivity Disorder', *Journal of the American Academy of Child and Adolescent Psychiatry*, 36 (12): 1715–1725.

Kuhnke, E. (2007) *Body Language for Dummies*. Chichester: Wiley.

Lee, C. (2004) *Preventing Bullying in Schools*. London: PCP.

Lee, J. (1993) *Facing the Fire*. New York: Bantam.

Long, R. and Fogell, J. (1999) *Supporting Pupils with Emotional Difficulties: Creating a Caring Environment for All*. London: David Fulton.

Lowenstein, L. (1978) 'Who is the bully?', *Bulletin of British Psychological Society*, 31: 147–149.

Mahony, T. (2007) *Making Your Words Work*. Carmarthen: Crown House.

Marland, M. (2001) 'School management and pupil care', *Pastoral Care in Education: An International Journal of Personal, Social and Emotional Development*, 19 (4): 25–34.

Mathieson, K. and Price, M. (2002) *Better Behaviour in Classrooms: A Framework for Inclusive Behaviour Management*. London: Routledge/Falmer.

Mehrabian, A. (1981) *Silent Messages: Implicit Communication of Emotions and Attitudes*. Belmont, CA: Wadsworth.

Moore, D. (2006) 'Education and Skills Committee – Minutes of Evidence: Oral Responses to Questions 1–47'. Available at www.publications.parliament.uk (accessed 10 May 2006).

National Association of Pastoral Care in Education (2005) 'Bullying and bystander behaviour in schools', *NAPCE Journal*, 23 (2).

Northern, S. (2004) 'A rotten way to feed the children', *Times Educational Supplement*, 16 April.

O'Regan, F. (2002) *How to Teach and Manage Children with ADHD*. Wisbech: LDA.

Osler, A., Street, C., Lall, M. and Vincent, K. (2002) *Not a Problem? Girls and School Exclusion*. London: National Children's Bureau.

Pease, A. (2000) *Body Language: How to Read Others' Thoughts by their Gestures*. London: Sheldon.

Pease, A. and Pease, B. (2002) *Why Men Lie and Women Cry*. London: Orion.

Prashnig, B. (2006) *Learning Styles in Action*. London: Network Educational.

Ready, R. and Burton, K. (2004) *NLP for Dummies*. Chichester: Wiley.

Ribbens, G. and Thompson, R. (2002) *Body Language in a Week*. Abingdon: Hodder and Stoughton.

Rigby, K. (2002) *New Perspectives on Bullying*. London: Jessica Kingsley.

Roffey, S. (2004) *The New Teacher's Guide to Behaviour*. London: Paul Chapman.

Rogers, B. (2004) *Cracking the Challenging Class*. Notes to DVD. Hendon: BooksEducation.

Schmidt, T. (1993) *Anger Management and Violence Prevention: A Group Activities Manual for Middle and High School Students*. Boston: Johnson Institute.

The Children's Society (2008) *Good Childhood Inquiry*. Available at www.childrenssociety.org.uk

Tuckman, B. (1965) *Developing Sequence in Small Groups*. Available at www.in-fed.org/thinkers/tuckman.htm

Tyrer, R. et al. (2004) *A Toolkit for the Effective Teaching Assistant*. London: Paul Chapman Publishing/Sage.

Vizard, D. (2003) *Behaviour Solutions for NQTs*. Available at www.behavioursolutions.com

Vizard, D. (2004a) *Fuel for Thought*. Available at www.behavioursolutions.com

Vizard, D. (2004b) *Teaching 14–16 Year Olds in Colleges of Further Education*. Available at www.behavioursolutions.com

Vizard, D. (2006) *A Guide to Syndromes and Conditions*. Available at www.behavioursolutions.com

Vizard, D. (2009) *Meeting the Needs of Disaffected Students*. London: Network Continuum.

Vizard, D. (2010) *A Guide to More Syndromes and Conditions*. Available at www.behavioursolutions.com

Wallis, C. (2004) 'What makes teens tick?', *Time Magazine*, 7 June, pp. 54–61.

Watkins, C. (1999) *Managing Classroom Behaviour: From Research to Diagnosis*. London: Institute of Education, University of London.

Wolf, A. (2011) *Wolf Review of 14–19 Vocational Education* (March), Professor Alison Wolf. London: DfE.

Wyatt, P. (2002) 'The rise of the alpha girls', *Mail on Sunday*, 24 March.

Starter activities/ideas

www.emc.cmich.edu/BrainBreaks/
www.mathisfun.net/magic.htm
www.ta-tutor.com – a Transactional Analysis website with puzzles e.g. Dingbats

Brain break ideas

www.braingym.org
www.brainbreaks.co.uk – free brain breaks and starter activities from Dave Vizard
www.quizardry.com

Other useful websites

www.behavioursolutions.com – articles and free newsletters on behaviour management issues
www.jlcbrain.com – Eric Jensen's Brain Learning website
www.kidscape.org.uk – a useful site on bullying
www.clc.co.nz – unique learner profiles, the website of Barbara Prashnig

THE ANGER ALPHABET

Understanding Anger – An Emotional Development Programme for Young Children aged 5-12

Second Edition

Tina Rae *Professional and Academic Tutor, University of East London*

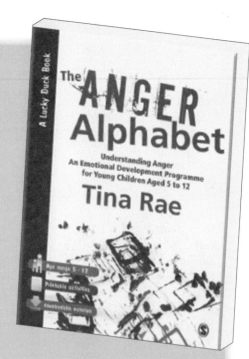

An ideal resource for primary teachers, this practical resource helps children understand anger and identify links with other emotions with an interactive programme using 26 elements. They will learn skills to effectively manage their anger with activities and exercises.

New to this edition is:

- information on recent initiatives on anger management in schools
- models and top tips for coping with anger
- new activities and ideas
- further information for young children aged 5-9

This instructional guide for teachers comes with photocopiable worksheets and activities suitable for both group and individual work for the whole-class which are available to download online.

CONTENTS

Introduction \ A Is for Anger \ B Is for Bottled-Up \ C Is for Cool It \ D Is for Dynamite \ E Is for Explosion \ F Is for Fuse \ G Is for Grumble Jar \ H Is for Helping Yourself \ I Is for 'I' Messages \ J Is for Joke \ K Is for Kettle Boiling \ L Is for Listening \ M Is for Move It \ N Is for No \ O Is for Outside \ P Is for Post It \ Q Is for Quality Talk \ R Is for Rules \ S Is for Shield \ T Is for Traffic Lights \ U Is for Understanding \ V Is for Vocabulary \ W Is for Wind Down \ X Is for X-Ray Eyes \ Y Is for Yell \ Z Is for Zero

READERSHIP
Primary teachers

LUCKY DUCK BOOKS

November 2012 • 160 pages
Cloth (978-1-4462-4912-3) • £70.00
Paper (978-1-4462-4913-0) • £25.99

ALSO FROM SAGE

CLASSROOM BEHAVIOUR

A Practical Guide to Effective Teaching, Behaviour Management and Colleague Support

Third Edition

Bill Rogers *Independent Educational Consultant, Victoria, Australia*

In this Third Edition of his bestselling book, Bill Rogers looks at the issues facing teachers working in today's classrooms. Describing real situations and dilemmas, he offers advice on dealing with the challenges of the job, and how building up a rapport with both students and colleagues can support good practice.

New to this edition are sections on:

- dealing with bullying
- teaching students on the autistic spectrum in a mainstream classroom
- working with very challenging students

New features included in the text are:

- a wider range of case studies, covering students aged 4 to 18
- questions for discussion
- a Glossary of key terms

Bill Rogers understands the demanding nature of the job, and offers wise words and inspirational encouragement to all those involved in educating our children and young people.

READERSHIP

Teachers, teacher assistants and newly qualified teachers

2011 • 280 pages
Cloth (978-0-85702-166-3) • £65.00
Paper (978-0-85702-167-0) • £22.99
Electronic (978-1-4462-0939-4) • £22.99

ALSO FROM SAGE

THE BEHAVIOUR MANAGEMENT TOOLKIT

Avoiding Exclusion at School

Edited by **Chris Parry-Mitchell**

Based on her successful work across a range of schools, this book consists of 10 sessions that make up a programme to help students who are at risk of exclusion. Each session has detailed facilitator notes and accompanying worksheets on the CD-Rom. The young people learn how to think, communicate, behave and relate to each other and other people in more useful ways.

The book offers:

- content that works for schools, Pupil Referral Units and any setting working with young people on behaviour management
- advice on dealing with common pitfalls and difficult scenarios
- guidance on how to work with parents and carers to help them understand how they can reinforce the approach at home
- activities that work with the 10 to 18 age range

Everything in this book has been tried and tested with young people who are at risk within their school settings, and for most of them it has been a turning point in their lives.

CONTENTS

How to Use This Book \ Points to Consider \ Session 1: Introducing the Toolkit \ Session 2: Games, Hooks and Tactics \ Session 3: What Makes Me Tick? \ Session 4: Hitting the Targets \ Session 5: Keep It Real \ Session 6: Lights, Action, Drama! \ Session 7: Fast forward \ Session 8: Step over Here \ Session 9: Premier Skills \ Session 10: Look at Me Now...

READERSHIP

Teachers and parents

LUCKY DUCK BOOKS

April 2012 • 160 pages
Cloth (978-1-4462-1074-1) • £90.00
Paper (978-1-4462-1075-8) • £30.00

ALSO FROM SAGE